TRAFALGAR SQUARE
A VISUAL HISTORY OF LONDON'S LANDMARK THROUGH TIME

TRAFALGAR SQUARE
A VISUAL HISTORY OF LONDON'S LANDMARK THROUGH TIME

JEAN HOOD

Foreword by Charles Saumarez Smith,
Director of the National Gallery

Batsford

For Judy, Peter and Sarah…
not just for Christmas

First published in 2005 by
B T Batsford
The Chrysalis Building
Bramley Road
London W10 6SP
www.chrysalisbooks.co.uk

An imprint of **Chrysalis** Books Group plc

British Library Cataloguing in Publication Data
A record of this title is available from the British Library

ISBN 0 7134 8967 7

Printed in China

Distributed in the United States and Canada by Sterling Publishing Co., 387 Park Avenue South, New York, NY 10016, USA.

ENDPAPERS Extract from the Ordnance Survey map of Charing Cross and Trafalgar Square, 1894–6. © Alan Godfrey.

FRONTISPIECE For over 160 years the statue of Lord Nelson has dominated not just the open space of Trafalgar Square but much of the Central London skyline. Nelson stares out across the Thames and past the London Eye; behind him, beyond the National Gallery, London stretches to the north where the horizon is punctured by the BT tower and Centre Point.

CONTENTS

ACKNOWLEDGEMENTS

This book could never have been written without a great deal of generous help and cooperation from the following archives, libraries, individuals and institutions in London and beyond: National Archives, British Library, National Maritime Museum, Manchester Central Library, Sandbach Library, Westminster Archives, Westminster Central Reference Library, National Gallery, St Martin-in-the-Fields, Canada High Commission, South Africa High Commission, Knight Frank, Drummond's Bank, Hugh Pearman, Royal College of Physicians, Ben McKnight, Greater London Authority, Socialist Worker, John on the 17.16 from Euston, Ken McNaught, Bill Woodrow, RIBA, Bill Rellstab, Henry Brownrigg, *Sunderland Echo*, Neil Herron, Bridgeman Art Library, Illustrated London News, Victoria and Albert Museum, British Museum, Royal Society of Arts, Professor Graham Parry, *Wandsworth Guardian*, Stephen Rubin, and the Canadian War Museum.

Thanks also to all those, especially Lee Jackson, who have uploaded so much information, not least a wealth of historical documents, on to the internet; significant websites are listed in the Bibliography. And thanks are also due to all the many authors, past and present, whose works, also cited in the Bibliography, were consulted in the course of research.

Singling out individuals is perhaps unfair, but I would like to express particular gratitude to Charles Saumarez Smith, Oliver Howard, Roger Shaljean, Jeff Peet, Jim Rennie, Jessica Collins, Lorna de Smidt, Jemma Street, Briony Kelly, Rachel Lloyd, Luci Gosling, Katie Simpson, Alison Wright, Paul Velluet, my husband George, my friends in the south, Judy and Peter Greenwood and Simon and Denise Turrell, with their much appreciated spare rooms, and Lesley Cummings for walking the dog.

None of this would have even come about without the team at Conway Maritime Press. I'm very grateful to John Lee for entrusting such a fascinating project to me; to Alex Myers who did a fantastic job tracking down images; to Lee-May Lim for her work on the design; and last, but by no means least, to my wonderful editor, Alison Moss, whose calmness and clear vision held everything together and with whom it was a joy to work again.

In a work of such broad scope it is impossible to treat subjects in the depth they deserve, and inevitably generalisations have to be made in the interests of brevity; that said, I accept full responsibility for any errors.

Jean Hood

FOREWORD

Each morning I walk up Northumberland Avenue from Embankment tube station and then diagonally across Trafalgar Square, past the statue of Henry Havelock, the evangelical defender of the garrisons at Cawnpore and Lucknow during the Indian Mutiny, past Landseer's great lions at the base of Nelson's Column, past the fountains designed by Edwin Lutyens just before the Second World War and the lugubrious bust of Admiral Cunningham on the south side of Sir Charles Barry's balustrade, up Norman Foster's steps, to confront the great portico of William Wilkins' National Gallery, the colonnade of which works so much better architecturally from close to than far away.

Since the space has been pedestrianised two years ago, Trafalgar Square has become a much more effective urban composition, providing the possibility of sitting out on the steps in the summer sun, as well as for tourists to be photographed at the foot of Nelson's Column. It is perhaps too often spoiled in its appearance by temporary festivals and the ephemeral rubbish they generate, but the combination of history, grandeur and public protest is part of the psyche of the Square.

Briefly, as one walks across the Square, one can transport oneself back to the old Charing Cross, before the demolition of William Kent's stables. One can imagine oneself standing at the heart of the old British Empire in a setting which was made into a public space by the combined efforts of John Nash and Charles Barry and chosen long after Nelson's victory at Trafalgar as an appropriate space to celebrate it. George Agar Ellis thought that the National Gallery, when it was founded in 1824, should be sited at 'the very gang-way of London'. My Trustees, when I was Director of the National Portrait Gallery, always liked the fact that the Gallery was on what they described as 'the processional route', a reference to the route that royalty has always traditionally taken since the days of Queen Victoria and Wellington's state funeral on their way from Buckingham Palace to St Paul's Cathedral.

Suffice to say, Trafalgar Square is a space which is redolent of British history, as well as the nearest approximation to civic space that London will allow. It has been written about many times, but it certainly deserves its own history, outlining its evolution architecturally, in celebration of the 200th anniversary of Nelson's great victory at Trafalgar in 1805.

Charles Saumarez Smith
Director, National Gallery

View (drawn & etched by J.T. Smith, Engraver of the ANTIQUITIES of London & Westminster) from the House of W. Tunnard, Esq. on the Bankside, adjoining the seite of Shakspeare's Theatre — on Wednesday the 8th January, 1806; when the remains of the great ADMI... Greenwich to Whitehall; comprehending not only the Vessels attending & the various other objects incident to that Procession: but also the principal Buildings, &c between the Monument & Saint Pauls, inclusive.

...vered with Black cloth. The Standard borne by Capt. Sir Fra. Laforey Bt. Supported by Lieuts. Barker and Antram; ... at Greenwich: Fourth Barge, cov. with blk. Cloth: Chief Mourner Sir Peter Parker, Bt. Adm...
...borne by Capt. Bayntun (in the absence of Capt. Durham) supported by 2 Lieuts. Rouge croix and Bluemantle, ... Adm. Lord Radstock: 6 assistant Mourners, viz. Adml. Caldwell, Curtis, Bligh, Pole.
... Second Barge, cover'd with black Cloth: Heralds of Arms, bearing the Surcoat, Target & Sword Helm and ... Vice Adm. Whitshed & Taylor, Adm. Orde (in the absence of Vice Adm. Savage) & Rear...
...untlet & Spurs of the deceased: The Banner of the deceased, as K.B. borne by Capt. Rotheram, supp. by 2 Lieut. ... Rear Adm. Drury, Douglas, Wells, Coffin, Aylmer & Domett. Train Bearer to the Chief
...ner, with the augmentations, borne by Capt. Moorsom, supported by Lieuts. Keys & Tucker. —— Third Barge, cov. ... acting for Norroy K. of Arms: The Banner of Emblems borne by Capt. Hardy, supported by Li...
...ret, black plumes, &c. Capt. Yule, Atkinson (Master of the Victory) Capt. Williams, Lieut. Brown & Parches.—— ... Commissioners of the Admiralty, their Barge, & immediately after, the City State Barge...
...Norroy, K. of Arms (in the absence of Clarenceux, indisposed) Union Flag: Attendants on the Body, while ... ly the Barges of several of the Companies of the City of London. The Engraver is signall...

Dear is the Triumph, where one breath must tell —
"Though Victory crown'd him, yet the Hero fell!"

"He was ever the defender of the Citizens, both in body &
"mind; and continued his love towards his countrymen, all his life".
Maccabees.

London, Feb. 15th 1806, published according to Act of Parliament, by J.T. Smith, No. 36, Newman Street.

THE DEATH OF NELSON

In the bloodstained and splintered aftermath of the Battle of Trafalgar with the stink of sulphur thick between the decks, exhausted men sat and wept, tears cutting trails through the soot that stained their faces. Many had been press-ganged or otherwise induced to join the Royal Navy; all were subject to poor conditions, appalling danger and harsh, sometimes capricious, discipline. Yet they were united in grief with the officers as the news of their Admiral's death spread around the fleet to overshadow the victory.

The crucial word is *their*. The navy loved Nelson. He was no saint and there was nothing soft about him, but he had the elusive charm that inspired affection and the famous 'Nelson touch' that gained him universal respect and a string of unequalled victories at sea. Trafalgar ensured British dominance of the oceans for more than a hundred years, and Nelson remains the standard by which the naval leader is judged.

News of that painful victory reached London in the very early hours of 6 November 1805 and by the evening word had spread well beyond the capital. The mood was one of passionate pride and grief and, even without a powerful media industry to orchestrate hysterical shows of public sorrow, Nelson's death plunged the whole nation into mourning. His dashing exploits had made him a popular hero to the man in the street, and the business community was profoundly grateful to him as the most high-profile representative of a Royal Navy which had allowed British merchantmen to maintain their most important trading routes.

Even before his body, preserved in a cask of brandy, reached England to be transferred to its coffin ready for a state funeral of epic proportion, the call for some lasting commemoration of his life had begun. A subscription fund was opened in London by William Sheddon and John Julius Angerstein, the latter a wealthy Russian-born Jew who had made his name through underwriting shipping at Lloyds of London. Angerstein was responsible for setting up the Patriotic Fund at Lloyd's by which the business community raised considerable sums of money, particularly for the widows and orphans of those killed serving in the Royal Navy. He was less successful in the case of the Nelson fund, which achieved just over £1300, an insufficient sum for any worthwhile memorial, and so the money was invested and all but forgotten.

London may not have rallied to the cause but the souvenir industry, already used to capitalising on Nelson's many victories, was quick to step up production, while across the country subscribers began to pledge contributions for local memorials.

The Funeral Car that carried Nelson's coffin from Whitehall to St Paul's had been designed to resemble HMS Victory, complete with gilded stern. The figurehead, now in the National Maritime Museum, represents Fame holding up a laurel wreath, echoing the Latin inscription on the canopy. During the funeral procession the streets were packed with mourners, the wealthier among them paying for places on specially erected stands. With the navy still engaged in the war, the only naval representation came from the officers and men of Victory and pensioners from Greenwich Hospital.

The Funeral Car,

IN WHICH THE BODY OF THE LATE
VICE ADMIRAL HORATIO VISCOUNT NELSON

WAS CONVEYED FROM THE ADMIRALTY TO ST. PAUL'S CATHEDRAL FOR INTERMENT,

ON JANUARY 9, 1806.

THE INSCRIPTION PLACED ON THE CAR.	THE INSCRIPTION PLACED ON THE COFFIN.
In Gold Letters, in front of the Canopy, the word NILE. On one side, the following Motto,— " HOSTE DEVICTO, REQUIEVIT." (Having conquered the Enemy, he is at rest.) Behind, the word TRAFALGAR. And on the other side, the Motto,— " PALMAM QUI MERUIT FERAT." (Let him bear the palm who hath won it.) The lower part of the Car was decorated with Escutcheons on each side, Between which were inscribed, on one side, the words, SAN JOSEF, and L'ORIENT : And on the other, TRINIDAD, and BUCENTAURE. On the Festoon below, on each side, the word, TRAFALGAR.	*DEPOSITUM.* *The Most Noble Lord HORATIO NELSON, Viscount and Baron Nelson of the Nile, And of Burnham Thorpe in the County of Norfolk, Baron Nelson of the Nile, and of Hilborough, in the said County. Knight of the Most Hon. Order of the Bath ; Vice Admiral of the White Squadron of the Fleet, and Commander in Chief of his Majesty's Ships and Vessels in the Mediteranean. Also Duke of Bronte, in Sicily ; Knight Grand Cross of the Sicilian Order of St. Ferdinand, and of Merit. Member of the Ottoman Order of the Crescent, & Knight Grand Commander of the Order of St. Joachim. Born September 29, 1758. After a series of transcendent & heroic Services, this Gallant Admiral fell gloriously, in the moment of a brilliant and decisive Victory over the Combined Fleets of France and Spain, off Trafalgar, 21st October, 1805.*

The honour of erecting the first monument went to Captain Joshua Rowley of Castletownend on the coast of County Cork. Using eight local masons and the 1200 men under his command, he constructed a simple arch in just five hours on 5 November (the news reached Ireland before England). Other provincial monuments followed. In 1807 the foundation stone of the Portsdown Hill column was laid, which was partly financed with donations of two days' pay by the men who fought at Trafalgar. The following year a column designed by William Wilkins and Francis Johnston was put up in Sackville Street, Dublin. Visitors could climb an internal staircase to a gallery by the statue of Nelson for a panoramic view of the city and beyond.

Despite the Irish struggle for independence, the memorial survived until 1966, although the street was renamed O'Connell Street. On the 50th anniversary of the 1916 Easter Rising, Republican activists managed to lay explosives, which toppled the Admiral's statue in the early hours of the morning; the damaged column was subsequently demolished. Local people had mixed feelings: politically, the column was a reminder of British rule, but it had become part of the architecture and was a convenient meeting place.

Given such public zeal, one might have expected the British Parliament to announce immediate plans to lay out a great square in honour of the battle and ornament it with a fitting memorial to the man who had fallen in the moment of his greatest triumph. It was not to be: the government had other financial priorities as the war dragged on for another 10 years.

Trafalgar Square only gained that name by a stroke of good fortune, and Lord Nelson would have to wait 38 years to enjoy a pigeon's eye view over the capital city of the country for which he had fought and died. For anyone who believes that the nineteenth century was somehow better at great showpiece projects than we are today, the story of Trafalgar Square will come as a revelation.

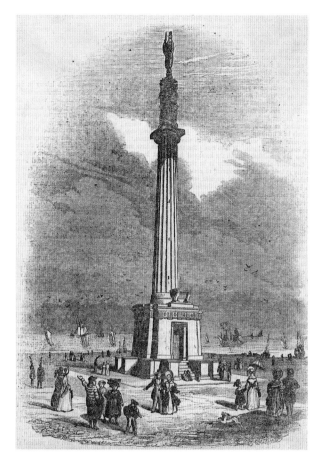

Erected in 1819 following a competition, the Great Yarmouth column was, like that in Dublin, designed by William Wilkins. This was fortuitous for the reputation of his illustrious rival, Sir Francis Chantrey, who had allowed enthusiasm to outstrip professional judgement in his design. Chantrey proposed a statue of Nelson 150 feet high. At night, the Garter Star could be illuminated to allow the memorial to double as a lighthouse. Wilkins hollow pillar stands 144 feet tall, and is crowned by the figure of Britannia. Visitors can climb the spiral staircase for a glorious view out to sea. The town had originally intended to commemorate the Battle of the Nile, but raising the necessary £10,000 took longer than anticipated.

In 1809 the merchants of Montreal commemorated the victor of Trafalgar with a column. The oldest monument in the city, possibly in Quebec, it stands in the Place Jacques Cartier and looks towards the later memorial to the eighteenth-century French naval commander, Jean Vauquelin, in the square named after him.

CHAPTER 1 THE ROAD TO THE SQUARE

Now that Trafalgar Square is so firmly established, literally and metaphorically, as the centre of London it is hard to realise that for many centuries the land on which it was built bordered the countryside that separated the City of London from the City of Westminster. Even with the aid of paintings and engravings it needs a massive feat of imagination to tear down the buildings, rip up the paving and tarmac, erase the idea of Northumberland Avenue and even demolish the Victoria Embankment in order to have any idea of what used to be there. Not for nothing was the church in St Martin's Lane known as St Martin-in-the-Fields.

Back in the seventeenth century, the City of London was the great centre of commerce, while the City of Westminster established itself as the seat of government. The two were linked by Fleet Street and the Strand, the latter taking its name from the old English word for the margins of a river, lake or sea. Until the building of the Embankment artificially increased its distance from the river, Strand ran quite close to the Thames. It was lined on the south side with the houses of the nobility, all with their river frontages for easy access by water to Whitehall and Westminster, and taverns, coaching inns and coffee houses also sprang up along this highway. But the most famous landmark, at the western end of the Strand, was an impressive cross built of Caen stone which had been erected several centuries earlier.

Charing Cross

In 1290, Queen Eleanor of Castile, wife of Edward I, died at Harby, a village near Lincoln. The genuinely grief-stricken King had her body embalmed and brought back to London to be interred at Westminster Abbey. The journey was slow, and Edward ordered that a cross should be erected in every town or village at which the cortege rested for the night. There were 12 in total, and the

OPPOSITE This is Trafalgar Square as it was until the recent pedestrianisation in front of the National Gallery, and it would be almost unrecognisable to the Londoner of Nelson's day. Three roads – Strand, Whitehall and Cockspur Street – have retained both their ancient names and routes; St Martin-in-the-Fields is the only original building to survive. In this aerial view, north is oriented to the left. Strand comes in from the east and meets Whitehall joining from the south and Cockspur Street which curves round to the west. Two major roads are linked to the Square from the west – Pall Mall via Pall Mall East, and The Mall, through Admiralty Arch.

RIGHT This extract from a map of London by George Braun and Frans Hogenberg from their book Civitates Orbis Terrarum, *published between 1572 and 1618, shows just how rural Charing Cross was at that time. Strand and Whitehall run parallel to the Thames as the river makes a 90-degree bend. The Eleanor Cross is visible at the intersection, and, to its right, St Martin's Lane runs north past St Martin-in-the-Fields.*

last stood at Charing at the junction of Strand, Cockspur Street and Whitehall.

There is a lovely tradition that the name Charing is a corruption of the phrase *chere reine*, French for beloved queen: at the time of the queen's death, French was still the language of the English ruling classes. Reality, however, is sadly unromantic.

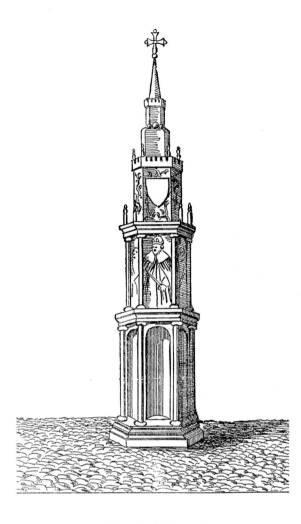

Of the original Eleanor Crosses only those at Waltham Cross, Geddington and Hardingstone remain. The monument that now stands in front of Charing Cross Station is an elaborate Victorian 'reconstruction' based on engravings of the original such as this, published in 1792.

Charing derives from a much older Anglo-Saxon word, *cerr*, meaning a bend in the river, and accurately reflects the course of the Thames at this point.

Charing Cross became a familiar marker for those making the journey between the two growing cities, and a useful meeting place. In 1647, as the English Civil War was coming to a close, it fell foul of the Puritans who, deciding it was a Catholic symbol, pulled it down, using the Caen stone to pave Whitehall, so trampling over the popery they feared and loathed.

The destruction of the cross did not pass without comment. A popular ballad, sung to the tune of 'Prince Rupert's March', lamented its passing:

> Undone, Undone, the lawyers cry and ramble up and down.
> We know not the way to Westminster now Charing
> Cross is down.
> [*Chorus*]
> Then fare you well old Charing Cross, then fare you well
> old stump.
> Thou wast a thing set up by a king and so pulled down
> by the Rump.
>
> The parliament did vote it down, a thing they thought
> most fitting.
> For fear its fall should kill them all in the House as they
> were sitting.
> [*Repeat Chorus*]
>
> The Whigs they do affirm and say on popery it was bent.
> For aught I know it may be so, for to Church it never went.
> [*Repeat Chorus*]

Had the Puritan iconoclasts been able to see into the future, they would probably have been outraged to know that less than 30

years later the site would be occupied by a statue equally unacceptable to their principles.

The statue of Charles I

The life-size equestrian statue of Charles I by the French sculptor, Hubert Le Sueur, which stands in front of the Square, has miraculously survived 400 years of turbulent history, from war and weather to riots and traffic. Equestrian statues of rulers go back to Roman times, but this was the first such representation of an English king, and it was also the most technically challenging piece of bronze casting ever attempted in the country up to that time.

Le Sueur based the horse on contemporary sketches of the King's 'great horses' by Sir Anthony Van Dyke who was painting large-scale canvases of the King on horseback, and there is a definite similarity between the statue and the two paintings of the King at Windsor Castle and in the National Gallery.

Cast in 1633, the statue had been commissioned by Richard Weston, 1st Earl of Portland, but he had only a couple of years in which to admire the magnificent work before he died, and by 1644 his Roehampton estate had passed into the hands of Sir Richard Dawes whose father had loaned money to the King. Two years earlier the English Civil War had broken out, and the tide was now turning in Parliament's favour. In January 1649 (1648 in contemporary documents since the New Year then began on 25 March) the King was executed and England became a republic. Royalist supporters such as Dawes found their estates seized, and the statue was ordered to be sold.

Three men from the Parish of St Paul's, Covent Garden, paid a derisory £150 for Le Sueur's masterpiece, and for a short time it enjoyed sanctuary in the churchyard. In 1650 Parliament decreed that Royalist statues at the Exchange and at St Paul's Cathedral should be destroyed; at the same time they enquired into the ownership of the Covent Garden statue. Nothing came of it, so the

Charles I, an excellent horseman and a man of personal courage, stood a little over 5 feet tall but Le Sueur's contract obliged him to add another foot. The King is portrayed bareheaded, wearing ceremonial black armour and carrying a marshal's baton.

RIGHT George Scharf sketched Charing Cross before the redevelopment. This passageway ran through the extensive stables and coach yards of the Golden Cross where, in 1800, a woman travelling on the Chatham and Rochester coach was killed after failing to duck under the low arch leading to Charing Cross.

OPPOSITE Thomas Shepherd provided an invaluable record of early nineteenth-century London. The Blackheath coach waits for passengers by the statue of Charles I, opposite the pinnacled entrance to the Golden Cross coaching inn. Northumberland House stretches away down the Strand, its famous lion standing sentinel.

statue was reprieved for a few years until 1655 when further enquiries were made.

At this point, facts begin to merge with legend. According to both, the statue was sold to a certain John Rivett, a brazier living not far away in Holborn, who was instructed to melt it down. Then, the story goes, unwilling to destroy this image of his late King he either buried it or hid it in the church vestry. To allay any suspicions, he proceeded to sell artefacts allegedly made from the metal, which were snapped up as relics by the defeated Royalists and as trophies by the Parliamentarians. At the Restoration in 1660 Rivett was able to produce the statue, to the delight of a grateful King Charles II, who appointed him King's Brazier.

In fact, Rivett was arrested at the Restoration and accused of appropriating Crown property. His defence, that he had bought it for its scrap value of £215 but without any intention of harming it, was believed. The statue was returned to the 2nd Earl of Portland and Rivett did indeed get his royal appointment.

Charles II ultimately purchased the statue and commissioned an ornate pedestal by Joshua Marshall (1629–1678), Master of the Mason's Company and Master Mason to the Crown. The Portland stone is now heavily weathered but when first made it was an excellent piece of work by one of the century's finest statuaries and it cost the King £230, £40 of which was for the shields, arms and trophies that decorate the front and the back. In 1676 the statue was symbolically erected on the very spot where the Eleanor Cross had stood.

Charles I now stares down Whitehall, scene of his own execution and, more pointedly, that of several of those who signed his death warrant. Perhaps it is the effect of hindsight, but Le Sueur appears to have captured something of the tragedy that the Italian sculptor, Bernini, found in the King's face and which Lionel Johnston later immortalised in poetry:

> Comely and calm, he rides
> Hard by his own Whitehall:
> Only the night wind glides:
> No crowds, nor rebels brawl.
> Alone he rides, alone,
> The fair and fatal king…

The growing city

As London expanded so Charing Cross became busier: here coaches and sedan chairs picked up and set down passengers; occasionally coaches crashed or overturned. Nelson's Column would eventually be raised on the site of the Golden Cross, one of

Night, by William Hogarth, 1738. Eighteenth-century Charing Cross could be rough after dark. At Rummer's Tavern and the Earl of Cardigan's Head locals celebrate the anniversary of the Restoration; the Salisbury Flying Coach has overturned in a street bonfire, and a maidservant escorts a drunken mason home. The overhead emptying of chamber pots provides an occupational hazard.

the busiest coaching inns in the city, certainly the biggest in the West End, and one that features in many novels, including Charles Dickens' *Pickwick Papers*. Its narrow, arched openings on to Charing Cross and St Martin's Lane disguised its size; it could stable 700 horses.

What also made Charing Cross famous, or infamous, depending on the point of view, was the pillory close by Charles I's statue, which regularly provided free public entertainment.

Compared to hanging and whipping, the pillory appears at first sight a mild punishment: humiliating but not life-threatening. In practice, it depended on the attitude of the crowd. In 1777 Ann Marrow was convicted of the unusual crime of 'going in men's clothes and personating a man in marriage with three different women'. The crowd, particularly the women, pelted her with such force that, unable to protect her face, she was blinded in both eyes. Daniel Defoe, however, met with a very different reception

The Charing Cross pillory could draw large crowds, augmented by spectators in overlooking buildings, to enjoy an hour or two of schadenfreude. Nash would soon demolish those to the right of the pillory; those to the left, including the tall Phoenix Assurance building, would later be swept away by Admiralty Arch.

The size of William Kent's magnificent Royal Stables can be gauged by looking at the horses and their grooms. Eventually demolished to make way for the National Gallery, it spent its last years as a store for government filing and a menagerie open to the public.

when he was sentenced to the pillory for seditious libel in 1703. He found his pillory garlanded with flowers and was given a rapturous welcome by the crowd who took the opportunity to display their anti-government feeling. Unable to persuade the public that persons guilty of sedition were criminals and not popular heroes standing up for free speech, the government eventually gave up using the pillory for such offenders.

Just south-east of the pillory and the statue stood Northumberland House, the London residence of the Dukes of Northumberland, built in Jacobean times and with the famous Percy lion overlooking Charing Cross from on high. To the north sprawled the King's Mews: two great courtyards separated by William Kent's Royal Stables. By 1805 the mainly wooden buildings forming coach houses and stores around the courtyards were dilapidated; not even the Royal Stables had been properly maintained. Not all of the Mews was given over to the Royal Stables, coach houses and ancillary services. A temporary barracks had appeared and the fire-engine horses of Phoenix

Assurance were also stabled on the southern side. Phoenix had been formed in 1781 by a group of businessmen involved in the sugar trade who were exasperated with the high cost of insurance and with the failure of underwriters to settle any claims in full. Four years later they established themselves at 57 Charing Cross, a stone-dressed building with Doric and Ionic columns opposite the Golden Cross where they were to remain for over a century.

Drummond's Bank

Another long-established business, and one whose name can still be seen, albeit on its rebuilt premises, was Drummond's Bank. Today it stands on the corner of Charing Cross and Admiralty Arch, not far from where, in 1712, a 24-year-old Edinburgh goldsmith named Andrew Drummond first set himself up in London at the sign of the Golden Eagle. Five years later he began a parallel career as a banker in one of six smart new brick houses alongside Northumberland House. His business did well: he and his successors became bankers to royalty, nobility and institutions such as Thomas Coram's Hospital for Foundlings. In 1758 Drummond's bought a plot on the opposite corner of Charing Cross, part of the site they still occupy. By the time Andrew Drummond died in 1769 his bank was making annual profits of almost £9000 and had close on 1500 accounts. By 1783 that profit had risen to £80,000 – a figure which, until they were brought to see the error of their ways, the partners spent on country houses. A more prudent regime allowed Drummond's to survive the great banking crisis of 1825 that sent panic through the country, and it emerged into the early Victorian era with a greatly extended building, a healthy balance sheet and a list of clients that read like Burke's peerage.

To the west of the Mews lay the Prince Regent's Pall Mall home, Carlton House, various gentlemen's clubs and St James's Park. Neither their presence nor that of businesses such as Drummond's made Charing Cross an exclusive area. To the north of the Strand and east of St Martin's Lane, including the parishes of St Giles and Covent Garden and the quarter known as Seven Dials, lived some of London's poorest. And the Prince Regent's favourite architect, John Nash, had plans for the area.

John Nash and the redevelopment of London

Nash enjoyed a chequered career but left the capital with arguably its most beautiful streets. After training under Robert Taylor he was desperately keen to make his mark in London but his first investment in the capital's property market bankrupted him. Undeterred he retreated to Carmarthen where he was not too proud to design the town gaol. Success in private house commissions, generally in the neo-medieval castle style, allowed him to return to London in 1795, where in 1798 he married Mary Bradley amidst some gossip as to whether she was the Prince Regent's mistress. In 1806 he was appointed architect to the Chief Commissioner of HM Woods, Forests and Land Revenues, which placed him in line for public contracts.

Admired by the Prince Regent; architect not just of the London Improvements but also the fantastical Brighton pavilion, he found his star in the ascendant until the fiasco over the spiralling costs of Buckingham Palace and the death of his patron ruined his reputation. In 1831 he retired to Cowes where he died four years later. He may not have laid out Trafalgar Square, but it is essentially his creation.

As early as 1793 the Surveyor General of HM Woods, Forests and Land Revenues had noted that leases on Mary-le-Bone Farm would end in 1811 and he recommended that long-term plans for that and other areas should be made in good time, but it was not until the eleventh hour that Nash came up with a radical scheme to develop what would come to be known as Regent's Park with its magnificent crescents and terraces. Not surprisingly, the Prince Regent was delighted with the plan, and with a few modifications the report was approved by the Treasury before the end of the year.

John Nash (1752–1835) came to define the architecture of a whole age: the Regency. He laid out more of London than any other architect, and Trafalgar Square owes its existence to him.

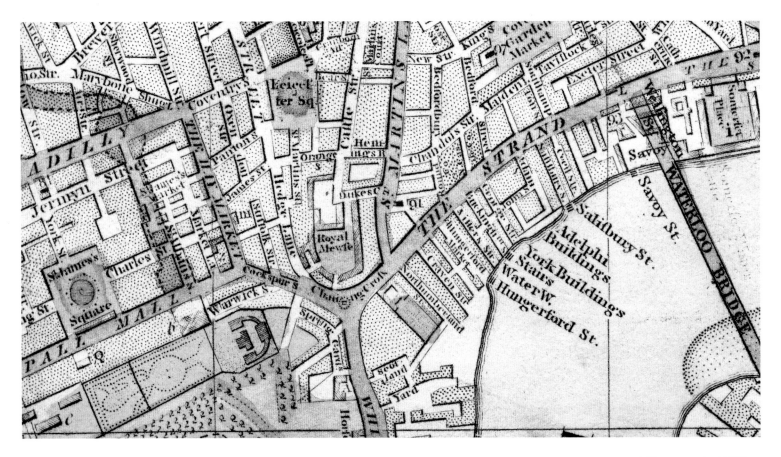

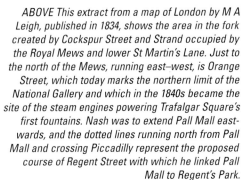

ABOVE This extract from a map of London by M A Leigh, published in 1834, shows the area in the fork created by Cockspur Street and Strand occupied by the Royal Mews and lower St Martin's Lane. Just to the north of the Mews, running east–west, is Orange Street, which today marks the northern limit of the National Gallery and which in the 1840s became the site of the steam engines powering Trafalgar Square's first fountains. Nash was to extend Pall Mall eastwards, and the dotted lines running north from Pall Mall and crossing Piccadilly represent the proposed course of Regent Street with which he linked Pall Mall to Regent's Park.

RIGHT Better known for his British Museum, Sir Robert Smirke (1781–1867) was the first architect to work on what became Trafalgar Square.

Nash further proposed the building of a new street (Regent Street) to run north–south and provide the Prince Regent with an elegant connection between Pall Mall and Portland Place leading to the new Regent's Park. 'It will quite eclipse Napoleon', the gleeful Prince reportedly told his friends. It would also, as Nash quite unashamedly avowed in his 1812 'First Report of H.M. Woods, Forests and Land Revenues', separate the homes of the gentry and nobility from those of the tradesmen and workers because there would be no access into the new street from the poor eastern side. It was a principle from which he refused to deviate.

Nash took an interest in the Charing Cross site. His vision was that the view down every significant street ought to end with a 'façade of beautiful architecture'. He looked at the way Whitehall sloped up towards the statue of Charles I and felt that if the statue were backed by a square or crescent opening on to Whitehall, it would 'afford a magnificent and beautiful termination' for anyone approaching it from the Whitehall direction. (In fact, the gradient that filled Nash with such enthusiasm would perplex subsequent architects.) Cockspur Street, so named because it was where the cock-fighting fraternity could purchase the spurs for their birds, was to be widened at Charing Cross, and Pall Mall would be extended eastwards along the southern side of Kent's Royal Stables. All this could be achieved by the demolition of the lower courtyard of the Royal Mews.

On 10 June 1813, King George III put his signature to 'An Act For Making A More Convenient Communication From Mary-Le-Bone Park And The Northern Parts Of The Metropolis To Charing Cross Within The Liberty Of Westminster And For Making A More Convenient Sewage For The Same'. Trafalgar Square was not yet visible on the horizon, but Nash was shaping a course towards it.

The Royal Mews was not the only potential casualty of Nash's vision. The people of St James's Market were successful in getting a Select Committee to enquire into their complaint that their livelihoods would be wrecked if they could not have access to New (Regent) Street, but their case was not upheld, nor was that of any group who asked for concessions.

Until the Mews was demolished, nothing could happen, which gave Nash time for additional thoughts about the space. In 1819 he revised his plan. Instead of having to dog-leg round both ends of the Royal Stables, Pall Mall East now extended only as far as the western end of the Stables; there was an open space in front of the Stables, and then a road left to join St Martin's Lane. The following year, it was agreed to relocate the Stables to Pimlico. Nash grew irritated about the delay in demolishing the lower courtyard, but he was about to take on another redevelopment: the rebuilding of Buckingham Palace for his royal patron, who in 1820 became George IV.

It should be stressed at this point that the area of open ground earmarked for the square was, mathematically, very far from being a square and that it was nothing like so large an area as was eventually developed. It represented, however, a clear beginning, and it was about to get its first tenants.

Nash was very clear that the buildings around his new square should house what he would have considered to be worthy institutions, such as the Royal Academy of Arts, the society founded in 1768 by George III to foster a national school of painting, sculpture and design; the Commissioners of HM Woods, Forests and Land Revenues were arguably more interested in rents. Fortunately, their interests coincided when the first leases, covering the western side of the square, were granted to the Royal College of Physicians and the Union Club; the first, a venerable institution with a charter already going back three centuries; the second, a recently founded gentlemen's club. These two would share what was, architecturally, a single building taking up one whole side of the square and designed by Sir Robert Smirke.

Smirke was one of the most influential architects of his day and a passionate devotee of the Greek Revival, which began in

This modern photograph of what, until 1925, was the Union Club shows the staircase hall to the right and the morning room, overlooking Cockspur Street, to the left. The two ground floor rooms with their scagliola columns, marble floors and fine plasterwork were combined during alterations for the Canada High Commission.

1804. During his travels he visited Athens just as Lord Elgin took down the marble frieze from the Parthenon. The experience dismayed him. 'It particularly affected me when I saw the destruction made to get down the basso relievos… Each stone as it fell shook the ground with its ponderous weight, with a deep hollow noise; it seemed like a convulsive groan of the injured spirit of the Temple'.

Smirke's 1809 rebuilding of Covent Garden Theatre in the plainest of the Greek styles, Doric, was widely copied, but by the 1820s he had moved on to the less stern Ionic, which can be seen not only in Trafalgar Square but, most famously, in his British Museum. However, although he was immensely successful, critics lament that his vision was too limited and his devotion too slavish to put him in the first rank of his profession.

One anonymous critic described the Trafalgar Square building as being severe to the point of dullness. Other commentators dubbed it dignified. The Pall Mall East frontage of the Royal College of Physicians consisted of a portico of golden Bath stone supported on six Ionic columns of Portland stone with their scrolled capitals also of the Bath stone. Inside the portico, two niches – later increased to three – held statues of three of the College's great luminaries, Thomas Linacre, Thomas Sydenham and William Harvey.

The main feature of the aspect of the building that forms the western side of Trafalgar Square is the recessed central portico, which draws attention away from the entrance to the Union Club. Right from the start it was all but impossible to see that there were two buildings.

The Union Club

Founded around 1800 to celebrate the Act of Union that added the Cross of St Patrick to those of St George and St David to create the Union Flag, the Union Club began its life in Pall Mall at the former Cumberland House, which had been reopened as a tavern appropriately named The Albion. It was a place where men gambled for high stakes and its 250 members were drawn from the nobility, the gentry, Members of Parliament and 'gentlemen of the highest respectability'. They included the playwright Richard Brinsley Sheridan, famous for comedies such as *The School for Scandal* and *The Rivals*.

The Union Club moved premises from Pall Mall first to St James's Square and then to Regent Street before deciding to re-constitute itself as a gentlemen's club in the more modern sense of the term – a quiet, luxurious place of meeting, relaxation and networking for an elite clientele. It would now seek members from the Church, members of both Houses of Parliament and, of course, respectable gentlemen whether titled or not. Clearly, solicitors failed to fall into any of these categories: they were barred until 1904.

The new home at Charing Cross cost them almost £24,000. A plan of 1903 shows capacious wine vaults in the basement, together with stores for beer, food, linen, coal and knives. Here, too, the housekeeper had her room, and there was an office for the steward, a hall where the servants could eat and a large kitchen. On the ground floor was the members' entrance into a large hall leading to the morning room with its rich pink scagliola columns.

Again by 1903, the ground floor included a coffee room and a strangers' dining room where non-members could be entertained, and upstairs there were smoking rooms for members and their guests as well as a library. The upper floors were reached by an elegant staircase with a banister down which a future Canadian High Commissioner would gleefully slide rather than use the stairs. Additions and alterations had been made to incorporate lifts and heating and to increase the accommodation, but the place was still recognisable as Smirke's building, despite an ugly raising of the height in 1852 which would not be the last.

The move allowed the Union Club to increase its membership to 800. Whereas a number of London clubs served the interest of political factions, the Union Club was apolitical and one of the first

OPPOSITE The King's Mews and the pillory have gone, and Smirke's building for the Union Club dominates the open space and the junction of Charing Cross and Cockspur Street. The Royal Stables, seen to the right of the statue, have yet to be demolished.

OPPOSITE On the right, opposite the Royal Stables, the northern elevation of Smirke's building shows the imposing Ionic portico of the Royal College of Physicians. Directly ahead stands the more decorative form of St Martin-in-the-Fields, visible for the first time from the newly-created Pall Mall East.

to admit gentlemen who had to earn their living, provided it was in one of the more acceptable professions such as architecture – Smirke was himself a member. It was considered to have a pleasant atmosphere, but not even the most easy-going institution could stand by when, in 1834, its pet cat was thrown from a top floor window by a scullery maid in the aftermath of a quarrel with one of the footmen. The cat died in the fall and the girl was sacked.

The Royal College of Physicians

The Royal College of Physicians' primary function was to set standards in medical practice. Its first attempts to establish a regulatory body came in 1511 when it successfully argued for an Act of Parliament to ensure that only qualified doctors and surgeons could operate within the City of London and a radius of 7 miles round it. Doctors within that circle had to be licensed by the Dean of Saint Paul's or the Bishop of London who would accept the recommendation of four qualified physicians or doctors. Beyond their jurisdiction, all doctors had to gain the approval of their bishop.

Seven years later, Henry VIII granted the Physicians their charter, which was subsequently ratified by an Act of Parliament. This development was not universally popular because, through the charter, the Physicians now insisted on examining all doctors, regardless of where they were trained. The man behind this important step was Thomas Linacre, who was anxious to establish an organisation along the lines of those in the Italian cities of Padua and Venice. The College's first premises consisted of two rooms in Linacre's own house, Stone Court, one for meetings and one for a library, which he stocked with his own books. On his death he willed Stone Court to the College where it remained until around 1614 when it leased premises at Amen Corner, near St Paul's Cathedral.

The Royal College of Physicians was fortunate in its benefactors. The site at Amen Corner was leased from the Church, and during the Civil War much Church land was confiscated by

Parliament. Dr Baldwin Hamey bought the lease and donated it to the College. In 1651 they gained a new library and museum funded by one of their most famous members, William Harvey, whose research into the circulation of the blood had revolutionised accepted beliefs. When fire destroyed the building, the Physicians purchased a building in nearby Warwick Lane from Dr Hollier, whose claim to fame has to be that he removed a bladder stone from Samuel Pepys. Originally designed by Robert Hooke, its Long Room was panelled for the Physicians with Spanish Oak paid for by Hamey.

In 1680 they were the beneficiaries of another generous gift, this time from the Marquis of Dorchester. Said to be the best unqualified medical practitioner in England, he had a superb library, and not just of medical and scientific works: his collection included an original copy of Chaucer's *Canterbury Tales* and the first book on dancing ever published. It was this collection that he donated to the College. Sir Christopher Wren was employed to make the necessary alterations to accommodate it, and afterwards the public were charged 3d (1.2p) to visit.

Although the building was, in itself, worthy of its owners, its location grew increasingly inconvenient. Its proximity to the expanding Newgate prison rather spoiled the Physicians' self-image, and as the eighteenth century rolled on more and more doctors were working in the lucrative West End. In 1799 they decided to move into Westminster. Such relocation required an Act of Parliament, passed in 1814.

John Nash offered them a lease on a building in Regent Street, but this was turned down, as were his drawings for premises in Charing Cross. The College was not in sound financial health and looking for help. In 1820 they set up a Building Fund and a letter was sent to the Home Secretary, Lord Sidmouth, asking for an interest-free loan of £20,000. This request was not as unrealistic as it might appear: precedents had been set by loans to the Royal College of Surgeons and the University of Edinburgh. The Physicians, however, were unsuccessful.

The Censor's Room has been reconstructed at the Royal College of Physician's Regent's Park premises and, with improved natural lighting, the quality of the oak panelling is more immediately striking than in the gloomier Pall Mall East days. Although not quite the same as before, the room has lost nothing of its intimidating ambience.

Halford Bt. His lordly personality, conservative views and architectural taste were believed to have influenced Smirke's design. Whether or not this is true, it certainly chimed with them. Perhaps more important for Smirke was the fact that he had to work with a site that, while quadrilateral, was not all right-angled and where the north–south axis sloped. And in the case of the Royal College of Physicians, Smirke had to accommodate his client's intention to import two of its most impressive rooms: the Dorchester Library and the highly important Censors' Room.

The Censors' Room might have been small but with its rich Spanish Oak panelling and the busts and portraits of men as famous as Hamey, Linacre and Harvey it was, and remains, a daunting place. It was in this room that, up to the 1830s, a young aspirant to the profession would take his final examination. Four eminent fellows – Halford had several times held the post of Censor – would orally grill him on his knowledge and pronounce his fate. Even worse must have been the disciplinary meetings held in the same intimidating surroundings.

On 25 June 1825 the College opened their new premises in a blaze of pomp in front of 5 princes, 5 dukes including Wellington, the Prime Minister, 13 lords and the society painter, Sir Thomas Lawrence. Afterwards the guests enjoyed a cold buffet, which Halford had paid for out of his own pocket.

The provincial doctor's son from Leicester had come a long way in a short time. Born Henry Vaughan he had practised at Scarborough for a few months before borrowing £1000 to set up his practice in Mayfair, and in 1793 he was elected Physician to the Middlesex Hospital and Physician Extraordinary to King George III. A Fellowship of the Royal College of Physicians was granted in 1794, in recognition of a meteoric rise to fame within his profession.

His patients included leading politicians such as William Pitt and three royal princes, and from 1800 he devoted all his time to a practice that was soon worth over £7000 annually. His wealth

The College decided to go ahead regardless by bringing together all the money it had and then borrowing £6000. At that point in time, politics abruptly turned in its favour and a long lease, worth £6000, was allotted in one of the new streets at Charing Cross. A grant of a further £2000 came from the Radcliffe Trust. Although the College had turned down Nash's design, they had been talking to another architect, Robert Smirke, and on the day that news of the grant came through, they celebrated by accepting Smirke's plan.

The force behind the decision to move to Trafalgar Square – more correctly, to Pall Mall East since the entrance to the building opened on to that street – came from the President, Sir Henry

was further increased when a distant relative, Sir Charles Halford, obligingly left him a large estate, as a consequence of which he changed his name to Halford. That same year, 1809, the King created him a baronet, and he was Physician in Ordinary for all four monarchs from George III to Victoria.

He held many positions within the College; most notably he was its President from 1820 for 24 years until his death. He made no great discoveries, but his diagnoses were good; he had an excellent bedside manner and he believed in being gently honest with families if he believed their loved ones were dying. His popular evening lectures drew audiences from far beyond the medical profession, and he ended the unfair practice of awarding Fellowships only to Oxbridge men.

The road to the Square

By the time the Royal College of Physicians and the Union Club had settled down in their new building, John Nash's plans had begun to proceed, albeit with a slowness that cast a blight over the whole area. The east and west sides of the lower Mews had at last been demolished and the soldiers in their temporary barracks relocated to Green Mews, the courtyard behind Kent's Royal Stables, which had themselves been vacated. The Commissioners of HM Woods, Forests and Land Revenues realised the potential of the site and their architect was asked to return to the drawing board and come up with a costed proposal for developing a plot that would extend much further east: right up to St Martin-in-the-Fields which, for the first time in its 100 years

John Nash's plan for the space in front of the Royal Stables, which he envisaged retaining, included the construction of a neoclassical building in the centre to house the Royal Academy and form a fitting backdrop to the statue of Charles I as viewed from Whitehall.

The businesses on the north eastern side of Charing Cross, from the Golden Cross to the lower end of St Martin's Lane, were among many scheduled for demolition around 1830. They include, centre, the Northumberland Coffee House, Dobree's pawnbrokers and two draper's shops. This became the south-east corner of the Square.

of existence, would be visible. Nash duly obliged and produced the first clearly recognisable plan of Trafalgar Square – although he envisaged an imposing building for the Royal Academy in the centre, equidistant from, and equal in length to, those on the east and west side.

The new plan required an Act of Parliament, which went through in June 1826, and was popularly referred to as 'The Charing Cross Improvements'. Not everyone was happy about what was going on. In April of that year a petition was presented to Parliament from 'certain tradesmen, leaseholders, yearly tenants and others, inhabitants of St Martin-in-the-Fields, whose property was to be taken'. They were dismayed because, so far, no one had discussed the subject of compensation. At the end of the year the term 'blight' was used in the House of Commons by the radical MP, John Cam Hobhouse. People in the area, he pointed out, were subject to 'severe and undeserved loss', because they were afraid to take in stock or make purchases and their tenure was so insecure.

from the steps of St Martins Church, august 1826

This Scharf view from the portico of St Martin's looks past the houses awaiting demolition – along with the Royal Stables – in order to make way for the National Gallery. In the distance, on the left, is the portico of the Royal College of Physicians.

On 8 April 1829 *The Times* reported a Commons discussion on the improvements at Charing Cross, where serious concerns were aired. One MP raised the matter of costs, claiming that the original estimates had been so moderate that Parliament had gone ahead without hesitation, believing that £400,000 would be sufficient. With the incorporation of other improvements this sum had risen to £851,213 0s 10d. As far as he was concerned, these costs were wide of the mark. 'Like most government undertakings', he told fellow MPs, 'this was a fallacy', and he suggested a figure of

£1,147,313 12s 9d. What bothered him was that after re-lettings had been taken into account, there would be a shortfall of close on £200,000. With a swipe at Lord Lowther, the minister responsible, he suggested with solicitous irony that perhaps the noble lord, like himself, had not managed to read through the mountains of paperwork produced by his department.

The MP also expressed concern at the effect the work was having on ordinary people. As reported in *The Times*: 'Extreme personal loss had been sustained in the whole of this district by

Scharf's 1826 drawing gives a marvellous impression of the crowded streets and courts around St Martin's Lane as seen from his house. The steeple of St Martin-in-the-Fields rises high above the rooftops, reminding us how closed-in the church used to be.

individuals who had been isolated by the demolition of buildings around them, and a butcher in that neighbourhood stated to him that his receipts in trade were diminished from £4,000 to £1,290 within the last three year'. Finally the MP had demanded that Parliament be given a breakdown of the more than £340,000 already spent on purchasing properties in the area.

All this disquiet was coming on top of the anger felt over the public money expended on Buckingham Palace. Nash's influence was waning. Others would take the new square forward after

William IV succeeded to the throne in 1830, and despite Nash's preference for 'worthy' establishments on the site, the eastern side had already been leased out and developed for housing.

St Martin-in-the-Fields

Although still without a name, the square had gained some form of physical definition from the two new buildings along the eastern and western sides and the Royal Stables to the north but there was no paving and nothing save John Nash's 1826 drawing to suggest what it might finally look like. The clearing of the area had, however, finally revealed to the public the view of a very attractive church at the north-eastern corner of the square: St Martin-in-the-Fields.

There had been a church on the site since at least the beginning of the thirteenth century, but by 1700 the building that stood at the southern end of St Martin's Lane, which had witnessed the baptism of Charles II and the funeral service for his mistress, Nell Gwynn, had been so enlarged and rebuilt that the structure had become unstable and no further repair was possible. From half a dozen competing architects, the Commissioners for Building Fifty New Churches in London chose James Gibbs, a closet Catholic whose London work had already established his church building credentials.

To be a Catholic in England after 1688 was risky, particularly for someone who depended on patronage for his commissions. Conversely, it was an advantage to Aberdeen-born Gibbs, when he went to Italy to study, making him the first British architect to have been formally trained abroad.

On his return, Gibbs found a kind and influential patron in the Scottish Catholic peer, Lord Mar, an enthusiastic amateur architect who recommended him for a vacant post as one of the Commissioners for Building Fifty New Churches in London. He was abruptly relieved of his post following his patron's involvement in the 1715 Jacobite uprising and his own denunciation as a Catholic, but he successfully begged to be allowed to complete St Mary-le-Strand.

For a while he worked only on private houses; then he was asked to finish the steeple of St Clement Danes. Commissioned for St George's Hanover Square and St Martin-in-the-Fields, he also designed the Radcliffe Library in Oxford, to which he left his papers and his own library. Ill health spoiled his later years, and when he died he left his whole estate to the son of his first patron, the Earl of Mar, in gratitude for his father's kindness to him.

James Gibbs (1682–1754), seen here in Rysbrack's 1726 portrait bust, may not enjoy the popular fame of Wren or Nash, but he has the distinction of having designed what his biographer Terry Friedman called, 'the most significant ecclesiastical building in the English speaking world'.

Gibbs longed to create the new St Martin's as a domed church but had to bow to financial constraints and the physical limitations of a site hemmed in by houses and shops and close to the Royal Mews. He revised his plans and came up with an elegant Italian baroque church that is certainly the finest piece of architecture on Trafalgar Square. In so doing, he came into line with the requirements of the Commissioners who wished all new churches to have the 'reverend look of a temple'. They even specified the provision of porticoes and demanded 'handsome spires rising in good proportion'.

Work began in 1721 and just over a year later the builders and masons had completed the foundations and were putting in the Portland stone bases of the 3-foot 4-inch Corinthian columns.

Whereas Smirke, a century later, would choose the Ionic column, Gibbs was about to show what could be tastefully achieved with the Corinthian with its much more elaborate capitals. By February 1723 the shell and inside works stood over 16 feet high, and in June 1726, with the interior of the building a hive of decorative activity, the scaffolding was struck. Consecration took place later that year, but it was another six months before the steeple was officially rung in. The building cost just over £33,000.

The most striking feature of the church is its portico. The eight smooth Corinthian columns of Portland Stone – the fossils of oysters can be seen in them – support a pediment carved with the royal coat of arms, and the theme of the columns carries on along the sides of the church but in the form of flat pilasters between the pairs of windows. Stone urns were intended to stand on the balustrade around the roof, each in line with a pilaster, but after a fatal accident involving such an urn at St Mary-le-Strand the idea was dropped. Gibbs put the larger windows above the smaller, which was unusual but necessary to accommodate the two seating galleries inside.

American visitors must feel a sense of *déjà vu* when they see St Martin's for the first time. Its influence, especially in the USA, has been enormous. Presidents Jefferson and Adams both admired it, and one has only to look at Jefferson's home, Monticello, and churches such as St Paul's New York and the First Congregational Church at New Haven, Connecticut, to recognise its importance.

The only pity, as the architect sadly noted at the time, was that nobody could ever stand back far enough to appreciate the beauty of his work. But when Nash did at last expose it, it leapt into favour, so much so that when another architect's plans appeared to threaten the new view, public opinion rallied to its defence.

Trafalgar Square

The outcry over St Martin's, however, was a few years into the future, by which time the square had at last acquired the name by which it would become famous across the world. If George Ledwell Taylor (1788–1873) is to be believed – and there is no reason to dispute his story other than the fact that William IV also claimed credit for the idea – he was the man responsible. However, it was generally believed at the time that the square would be named after the new king.

Taylor is an interesting character. Architect, surveyor, antiquarian and archaeologist, three or four times married and the father of 11 children by one of his wives, he made a 7000-mile Grand Tour of Europe with his lifelong friend, Edward Cresy, more than half of which was covered on foot. By 1830 he was developing the eastern side of Nash's square for housing – flats, he called them – and just as Smirke had contrived to make two buildings look, from the outside, like one, so Taylor's neoclassical block of apartments was uniform and also ornamented with groups of Ionic pilasters. The main entrance, opposite that of the Union Club, was covered by a small raised portico with a single, unassuming flight of stairs on the left-hand side. At the northern end the block rose five storeys above street level; by the southern end a lower-ground floor was completely exposed. Like Smirke he, too, had to contend with an irregular site pointing towards the statue of Charles I, and he chose to arrange the windows of the south elevation so they would echo those of the Union Club across the square. Financially, the development was a failure, and within a couple of years the building became Morley's Hotel, conveniently taking the place of the old Golden Cross coaching inn. Until 1920 it was a popular place to stay, both for travellers from around the world and for the fictional creations of popular novelists.

According to Taylor's autobiography, his first tenant wanted to have his visiting cards printed and needed to know what his address would be. Armed with his plans, the architect went to St James's Palace to ask for an audience with the recently crowned king – William IV – who, as a young prince serving in the Royal Navy, had been one of Nelson's friends.

OPPOSITE The barrel-vaulted roof of St Martin's, decorated with exquisite Italian plasterwork, appears to spring from the Corinthian columns and it provides a wonderful acoustic that still thrills audiences who flock to services and candlelit evening concerts. The glass of the altar windows was blown out during the Second World War.

I found other officers waiting, among them Sir Thomas Hardy [Captain of HMS *Victory* at Trafalgar].

'Ah, Taylor, what are you here for?'

'A private matter, Sir Thomas.'

However, while we were waiting, a thought struck me if I could get Sir Thomas to moot this subject, in whose arms Nelson died! So I addressed Sir Thomas, and told him my object adding: if he would be so kind as to make the suggestion to his Majesty.

'What,' said he, 'what do you take me for? To ask the King, who has consented to its being called after his own name?

Are you mad? I wish you well through it. I will have nothing to do with it.'

Notwithstanding this unpropitious opinion I awaited my time, and was before the King. I had some difficulty in opening my case, but His Majesty took most kindly to my arguments and said: 'I like the idea, let it be called Trafalgar Square. Go and tell Lord Duncannon so from me!'

Here was an awkward situation. I said: 'Your Majesty, I am but an humble man, unauthorised to convey such an order.'

'I see,' said His Majesty, 'give me your plan – pen and ink.' He wrote: Trafalgar Square – William Rex.

CHAPTER 2 ART AND ARCHITECTURE

The National Gallery

Surely nobody who has spent a couple of days at the National Gallery can have any complaint about the collection, other than the universal lament that a favourite painting is in another country's collection! But when it comes to the building that houses the treasures, controversy and criticism have been the order of the day for almost 200 years.

In 1824 London could claim for the first time to have a national art collection on permanent public display. It consisted of 38 paintings, all purchased from the estate of the late John Julius Angerstein (1735–1822), the man who had been behind the first attempt to raise money for a Nelson monument in London. Despite a lack of education, which, combined with his birth and his occupation, put him beyond the pale as far as Society was concerned, his taste in art, guided by the painter, Sir Thomas Lawrence, was good. While some of his paintings have been re-attributed to 'follower of' or 'studio of' the great masters with whose names they were originally credited, the collection was a fine start, including as it did Piombo's *The Raising of Lazarus*, Rembrandt's *The Woman Taken in Adultery* and *The Adoration of the Shepherds*, and Raphael's *Pope Julius II*.

The Treasury Minutes record that to purchase the collection would cost £57,000, and to open it to the public for a year would require a further £3000. This would pay for the remainder of the lease on Angerstein's former home at 100 Pall Mall and the cost of staff to take care of paintings and visitors.

The new gallery's purpose was best summed up by a young MP, George Agar Ellis, later Lord Dover, in a speech to Parliament. Acknowledging that going on the Grand Tour was beyond practically everyone in the country, irrespective of income, he went on to say that the only chance for most people of seeing 'what is really fine in art' was the establishment of a National Gallery. He believed passionately that 'the minds of all who are not entirely dead to the feelings of pictorial beauty will naturally be turned to the study of art, at the same time that their taste will be regulated by a just and proper standard of excellence'.

Agar Ellis then went further, demanding: 'no shutting it up half the days in the week; its doors must always be open, without fee or reward, to every decently dressed person… It must be situated in the very gang-way of London'.

The new institution, already enjoying significant numbers of visitors, appealed successfully for donations of paintings to increase its collection: two years after opening, its first catalogue listed 76 paintings, including a bequest by Sir George Beaumont who, some months before Angerstein's death, had offered his own collection to the nation once a purpose-built gallery was provided. And as it outgrew the premises that some visitors considered dark and dingy, unflattering comparisons were made between London's leading art gallery and that of its great rival in Paris, where, then as now, the French national art collection enjoyed the palatial splendour of the Louvre.

Wilkins' gallery

William Wilkins (1778–1839), the architect responsible for the Great Yarmouth monument to Nelson, and, like all architects, anxious to enjoy a slice of the very rich cake that Nash's ideas for London had produced, wrote to the Trustees in 1831. He outlined a plan to replace the Royal Stables at the newly christened Trafalgar Square with a building to accommodate both the National Gallery and the Royal Academy. At that particular time the Commissioners for HM Woods, Forests and Land Revenues, understandably concerned with the balance sheet, had been considering leasing the north side for commercial development, but by 1832 both parliamentary parties had recognised the social possibilities of art for all. A National Gallery would help to unite rich and poor,

OPPOSITE The next 15 years saw the laying out of Trafalgar Square and the two edifices that would bring it international fame: The Nelson monument and the National Gallery, which today houses one of the greatest collections of European art anywhere in the world. For the past century the National Gallery has hung its paintings in a single row so that admirers can enjoy each one without distraction or a stiff neck. Visitors to the Gallery's first home at 100 Pall Mall were not so fortunate. Frederick MacKenzie's 1834 watercolour shows the crowded principal room which is dominated by Sebastiano del Piombo's The Raising of Lazarus.

Nº 100, PALL MALL,
or the National Gallery of England.
To The
Right Honble Charles Earl Grey.
FIRST LORD OF THE TREASURY &c &c &c.

ABOVE LEFT AND RIGHT Pressure for a National Gallery really began in 1823. Hardly had 100 Pall Mall been secured than comparisons with the Louvre began, accompanied by a quotation from Shakespeare's Hamlet *to emphasise London's inferiority to Paris: 'Look here upon this picture, and on this; The counterfeit presentment of two brothers'.*

educated and uneducated; and if 'music hath power to soothe a savage breast', as dramatist William Congreve claimed, art might soften angry and antisocial feelings among the more disadvantaged in society.

Four architects, including Sir Robert Smirke and John Nash, were invited to submit designs, but it was the handsome, wealthy and scholarly social aspirant, Wilkins, whose design was selected.

Wilkins' father's success as a building contractor had enabled him to give his son a Cambridge education. The results of a subsequent two-year bursary to study classical remains in Sicily and Greece earned him a Fellowship at Gonville and Caius College and confirmed him in his enthusiasm for Greek architecture,

although he also designed in other fashionable styles. Successful as both architect and scholar, he also inherited a string of theatres in East Anglia from his father.

He worked on a number of Cambridge colleges, including the critically acclaimed Corpus Christi, and implemented the most enlightened social thinking at the new Norwich Gaol. He then moved to London where his most admirable building was University College. A generally popular man, he could be staunchly opinionated on occasion and a little lacking in modesty, qualities which would not endear him to his critics.

For the National Galley he proposed, and in 1833 exhibited a model of, a building 56 feet wide and 461 feet long – considerably

This painting commemorating the wedding of Prince Edward, later Edward VII, and Princess Alexandra on 7 March 1863 allows a reasonable comparison between the National Gallery and St Martin-in-the-Fields, which Wilkins had wished to obscure. John Constable called the Gallery 'a very noble house' but he was in a tiny minority. A letter-writer to The Times castigated 'that monument to public economy yclep'd [named] The National Gallery' and in 1842 the Illustrated London News claimed that St Martin-in-the-Fields 'is admired by everyone possessed of any taste and now has the advantage of standing in contrast with the National Gallery, a building which no one of any taste can admire at all'. Wilkins was mercifully spared much of the vituperative criticism: he died in 1839 at the age of exactly 61 having lived to see his work inaugurated in 1837 by one monarch and officially opened in 1838 by another.

longer than the Royal Stables. He also looked at the shape of Trafalgar Square and decided that he would bring his building forward and angle it slightly in the interests of symmetry. In so doing he would have to obscure the portico of St Martin's church, which had so recently been opened to view across the Square. Admirers of James Gibbs' masterpiece were immediately up in arms, demanding that the Gallery be moved back. Unwisely, Wilkins put pen to paper and early in March 1833 published a pamphlet to justify his proposal.

Having begun by the reminder that if it had not been for his plans the site would have been occupied by *a line of shops and dwellings* [Wilkins' italics]', he turned his attention to some of the contracts entered into between the Crown and the Parish of St Martin's, but then he made the first of several mistakes of tone. Referring to the complaints that his edifice would exclude the front view of St Martin's from Pall Mall East, he declared arrogantly: 'Only the layman could think St. Martin's a fine piece of architecture'. He criticised the distance between the columns and

called the pediment above 'of prodigious, unnecessary and unexampled height'. Worst of all, in his opinion, Gibbs had put a Gothic spire on a Greek church. Then he added condescendingly that if the public had to look at the church obliquely, as his plan intended, 'all these horrors are resolved and the effect, in spite of the spire, is really beautiful'.

What obviously irritated him was that things had gone from one extreme to the other. For a century the church had been hidden and nobody had complained; now, suddenly, it had to be kept visible at all costs. 'I cannot affect a false humility', he assured his critics, '…I should have passed a great many years of useless study if I could not design something very superior to that of St. Martin's Church'.

After further carping that the Church was based on the architectural principles of Vitruvius, which he deplored as unfaithful to the Grecian ideal, he ended with a flourish, predicting that, although St Martin's was too big to be ignored, it would become subordinate to his National Gallery. 'I know this to be true,

For the duration of its construction, a hoarding was placed in front of the National Gallery. It was quickly covered with adverts, providing information and amusement for passers-by. Competition among the freelance advertisers even lead to violence. The picture can be dated 1836 by the advert for Jump Jim Crow *playing that year at the Adelphi Theatre.*

and knowing it, I express it… I may be called vain, and I shall certainly be thought so'.

He was.

Some of his critics went public, including Charles Purser and Joseph Gwilt FSA FRSA. The latter had translated Vitruvius and took great pleasure in pointing out that Vitruvius, the inspiration behind the great Italian architect, Palladio, was in any case Roman, not Greek. But what worried both men was a fear that Wilkins' Gallery was just not going to be good enough. Feeling that the £50,000 allotted by Parliament was ridiculous, 'no more than a gentleman would spend on a mansion for himself', Gwilt advised that the project should be postponed until there were sufficient funds. The alternative would be regular injections of public money. Purser said of the proposed Gallery: 'Ill suited to the wants of our present age, it is still less adapted to meet the needs of posterity…will become another national blunder…erected in one reign to be abandoned in the next'.

Purser advocated siting the Gallery somewhere else entirely where it would be easier to build future extensions, and in March and May 1833 *The Times* made a similar point, favouring Regent's Park, and also deploring any idea of the Gallery sharing its space with the Royal Academy.

As late as August 1833, Lord Duncannon, in charge of the Commissioners of HM Woods, Forests and Land Revenues, replied to a question in the House of Commons on the continually rising costs of the building, which, the questioner feared, might exceed £70,000. Duncannon answered that given the costs and the furore over St Martin's there might be an argument for scrapping the project. The alternative was to house the National Gallery in the Banqueting Hall in Whitehall, keep a good space open in front of St Martin's, pay Wilkins for his plans and lease the Trafalgar Square site for building. Nothing came of this, but Wilkins' building was moved back some 40 feet. Fears that the money was inadequate for the project were not groundless: a number of economies had to be made, including the use of reclaimed materials from the now-demolished Carlton House on Pall Mall which reduced the 1833 estimate of £66,000 by some £4000.

Misgivings notwithstanding, work on the building went ahead. It was designed as two wings, the western wing designated for the records and administrative work of the National Gallery. Above these offices, and lit by natural light from the huge lantern-roofs, were the four main picture rooms and four cabinets suitable for smaller works. Until 1869 the Royal Academy resided in the eastern wing with a hall for casts, a library and the Council Room. The drum beneath the central dome was the Royal Academy's drawing studio.

Wilkins was working under almost impossible conditions. He was constrained by a parsimonious Treasury into using not only the Corinthian columns of Carlton House, but also some of the sculpture left over from the building of Marble Arch. The columns proved too small for the central portico, but it is thought they might have been used in the smaller east and west porticoes. His plan for a grand flight of steps on all three sides of the portico was also scrapped, leaving the Gallery with a high blank wall facing the viewer and access only by stairs at either side. He had to give space for the view of St Martin's, provide open access routes through the building for the soldiers stationed in the barracks behind, on whose land he could not encroach, and accommodate two institutions on a limited site. The result was, as the critics had predicted, insufficient in the medium term, never mind the long term, since pictures could only be exhibited on the top floor where they could receive natural light.

While the National Gallery was under construction, its future tenants, their ranks swollen by additional donations, had to move into 105 Pall Mall as their original home was due for demolition.

At the end of the century George Augustus Sala recalled one aspect of the Gallery's construction in 'Three P.M.: At the National Gallery'.

The centre of the new building was shared between the two institutions and designed to look impressive with its staircases and halls. It was to be, as the Treasury Report stated: 'distinct and separate but so brought together as to form one grand feature of interior decoration'.

In the year 1836 we were living in King Street, St. James's, opposite St. James's Theatre. Trafalgar Square was then being laid out, and the area was surrounded by an immense hoarding, which, notwithstanding minatory notices of 'Stick no Bills,' and 'Bill-Stickers, Beware,' was continually plastered over with placards relating to all kinds of things, theatrical and commercial, and at election time with political squibs. There were in those days no bill poster advertising-contractors. The bill-stickers were an independent race, whose main objects in life were first, to get a sufficient number of bills to stick up, and next, to cover over the placards pasted on the hoardings by their rivals. Thus the perpetually superposed bills led to a most amusing confusion of incongruities. If you tried to read, say, six square yards of posters, the information was conveyed to your mind that Madam Malibran was about to appear in the opera of Cockle's Pills; that the leader for Westminster was the only cure for rheumatism; that Mr. Van Amburg and his lions would be present at the ball of the Royal Caledonian Asylum; and that the *Sun* evening newspaper would contain Rowland's Maccassar Oil; two hundred bricks to be sold at a bargain; and the band of the Second Life Guards would be sure to ask for Dunn's penny chocolate at the Philharmonic Concert, with Mademoiselle Duvernay in the Cachuca.

Most prestigious building contracts are controversial but in the case of the National Gallery hardly anybody had a good word to say about it, and Wilkins' assertion that it would cast St Martin's into the shade must have come back to haunt him during the last two years of his life. When the Gallery opened to the public in 1837, *The Times* was scathing about both the interior and the exterior: 'The contemptible closets of the pie-crust edifice'. (Then again, it was also unimpressed with some of the recent acquisitions, calling Constable's *Cornfield*: 'clever but partaking too much of the eggs and spinach style of colouring to resemble the vegetation of an English landscape'.) *The Architect, Engineer and Surveyor* referred to the Gallery in 1841 as: 'The thing upon the north side of Trafalgar Square sometimes called the National Gallery and sometimes the National Pepper boxes', and returned to the attack in 1843: 'Much has been said about the National Gallery's meanness of design and its indescribable detail; for no sufficiently degrading adjective has yet been discovered to characterise the features of our national depository of art'.

The basic problem was that the building simply lacked the grandeur required by the site, and that lack of presence was accentuated by the slope up to it. Wilkins had tried to remedy this by raising the whole building 12 feet above street level, but the result was to increase the height of the blank wall below the central portico. However, he did ensure the inclusion of several practical features, which his critics ignored. One was the use of cast iron in the construction, rather than wood, to reduce the risk of fire; another was the provision of large trapdoors in the floors so that paintings could be moved easily and with less risk of damage. His lantern roof of glass panes set into iron frames and with adjustable ventilation, was extremely advanced, if unprepossessing from the outside, and demonstrated his readiness to marry modern technology with classical design.

Once open, the National Gallery began to fulfil its mission to bring art to the people. In January 1844 the *Illustrated London News* reported on a visit by 200 boys from the Marylebone Workhouse. Each child had to follow close behind the one in front

Once the steps to the National Gallery have been climbed, any aesthetic disadvantages are forgotten, and the elevated central portico gives the finest view across Trafalgar Square available to the general public – as these Edwardian visitors have clearly discovered. It also offers a second attractive view: eastwards to St Martin-in-the-Fields whose Italianate spire is perfectly framed by Wilkins' columns. It has been said in defence of Wilkins that he did not design the Gallery to be viewed from Whitehall; rather, he thought more of the view from Pall Mall East towards St Martin's. After all, Nash's plans for a magnificent view from Whitehall had depended upon the Royal Academy occupying a central space nearer the southern edge of the Square. If we take into account Wilkins' active involvement in the theatre, it becomes easy to see the three buildings – the Gallery, the church and the entrance to the Royal College of Physicians as three 'flats' in an open-air stage set.

The National Gallery's educational outreach programme began at the start of Queen Victoria's reign. This 1870 party of working men appears keenly interested in what the enthusiastic guide is saying. Notice how the paintings are still crowded together and how, as now, the public is allowed very close.

while 'encircling with his left arm the rail which prevents a too-near approach to the pictures' and the group was told to 'look over their left at the pictures'. Nobody thought to ask the boys for their opinions or what, if any, connection they could make with the paintings. Commentators differed as to how much interest the working classes took in the paintings, but they were united in praising their behaviour.

Architecture aside, the National Gallery was a growing success, with visitor numbers increasing until by 1844 there were around 50,000 per year, four times as many as in 1837.

The Nelson Memorial Committee

With the buildings complete, the Commissioners addressed themselves to the question of the Square itself, still without a paving stone to its name. They had Nash's plan and also one drawn up by Wilkins in 1837. The latter proposed levelling the site and creating a terrace in front of the maligned National Gallery, but before anything could be done a committee of well-connected persons obtained permission to put a very large monument on the site.

Back in June 1834 a letter-writer in *The Times*, asking what was going to be done with Trafalgar Square, revived memories of Sir Francis Chantrey's rejected entry for the Great Yarmouth monument to Lord Nelson. Fortunately for both Chantrey and London, the suggestion, like the statue, failed to get off the ground. Nevertheless, the anonymous writer was not the only one who felt that Nelson had been neglected for too long.

The Thatched House tavern in fashionable St James's Street was the venue for an important gathering on 22 February 1838, chaired for the interim by Admiral Sir George Cockburn and including Sir Thomas Hardy. This was the first meeting of the Nelson Memorial Committee and it resolved to erect 'a National Monument in a conspicuous part of the Metropolis'. If the words 'Trafalgar Square' did not appear in the resolution, they cannot have been far from the men's minds. The Committee was considered a temporary one, its first tasks being to bring on board as many rich and influential people as possible and open a subscription fund.

In this they were very successful, gaining the support of Lord Melbourne, the Prime Minister, and Thomas Spring-Rice, the Chancellor the Exchequer, as well as senior ranks from the navy and a substantial percentage of the most highly-titled men in the land. The Dukes of Wellington and Buckingham had both indicated their willingness to join the Committee and at a meeting on 26 March, again at the Thatched House, a resolution was moved 'to make every possible endeavour to obtain a space of ground in Trafalgar Square'. Captain Sartorius summed up the general hope by extolling Trafalgar Square as 'the noblest site that could be given in the first metropolis of the world'.

The Committee asked its members to approve the sending of invitations to all artists who expressed an interest in submitting designs. The Chairman's observation that since foreign artists were permitted to compete information should be published in the French and German press, drew fire from the plain spoken John Wilson Croker who felt that inviting the French to compete would be enough to make Nelson rise from his grave.

At the meeting on 11 June the chairman of the permanent Committee, the Duke of Buccleugh, was able to report that the Trafalgar Square site had been granted with the expected proviso that the design should be approved. He also drew the audience's attention to the existence of the fund opened by John Julius Angerstein after Nelson's death, which had been left to accrue interest and had been offered to them. £1380 had risen to £5510, a good sum with which to open the subscription.

The atmosphere that night was celebratory. Eulogies of Nelson, a donation of £500 from Queen Victoria and a proposal to exhibit all the competing plans for the monument met with cheers that ranged from loud to ecstatic. In the light of much later public discussion as to whether Trafalgar Square should have honoured only naval heroes, it is interesting to note that the Committee loudly applauded a suggestion that it should commemorate naval and military men. With the Duke of Wellington present anything else might have seemed impolite. But the speaker was making a point. Poets, artists and politicians had their place in Westminster Abbey; Trafalgar Square should be for the men who took up arms for queen and country.

The competition

The closing date for the submission of designs was just 30 June, and prizes of £300, £150 and £100 were to be awarded to the first, second and third placed entries respectively. With no real idea of

the amount of money they would have at their disposal, the Committee asked entrants to cost their designs and aim to stay between £20,000 and £30,000. It is an interesting sum, given that the government had optimistically hoped to complete the whole National Gallery project initially for £32,000 and then for no more than £50,000.

The timescale caused consternation and a flood of complaints from those practitioners working abroad, so the Committee decided to re-advertise the competition, extending the deadline to 31 January 1839. This highly prestigious commission attracted a very large entry from well-known architects and sculptors and from those hoping to catapult themselves to fame. Plans began to flow in, to the discomfort of Charles Scott, the son of the Reverend Alexander John Scott, Nelson's Secretary, to whose office they were all addressed. They amounted to some 140, many accompanied by scale models.

The Committee had promised that all plans and models would be displayed, and were offered premises in Regent Street at the former home of John Nash. They had also convened a panel of judges drawn very much from their own ranks, which included Wellington, the Chancellor of the Exchequer, Admiral Cockburn and the Earl of Cadogan. The idea of inviting eminent artists to make or contribute to the decision had obviously not been considered, which would provoke the anger of the artistic establishment.

The task of putting a memorial in such a large and public place taxed the ingenuity of the entrants. Full of patriotic fervour, they allowed the words 'simplicity' and 'taste' by and large to vanish from their vocabulary. The Chester architect, James Harrison, proposed a temple to the navy containing a 'colossal statue of Nelson, around which are receptacles for the statues of future naval heroes as they arise. The sixteen statues under the porticoes are of the admirals of England'. Above each statue was to be a bas relief illustrating the subject's finest hour, and the pediment of the

Compare William Railton's winning design for the Nelson monument with the actual column and one major difference is obvious: Railton planned a flight of steps on each side to lead up towards the base of the column. For financial reasons they were never built.

The detail of Railton's proposed column shows the elaborate capital decorated with acanthus leaves that characterises the Corinthian order of architecture, the fluted shaft and the square base with the low relief (bas relief) sculptures of Nelson's great victories. The three people provide the necessary sense of scale.

portico was to be 17 feet wider than the National Gallery's central portico. If that was not enough, this temple was to be surmounted by an obelisk taking the monument to 100 feet, higher than the dome of the National Gallery. Harrison proposed decorating the whole with fountains in the form of crocodiles and lions, huge statues symbolising Nelson's great battles and sculpture representing, not just the biography of Nelson but, funds permitting, the history of the Royal Navy as well. With honesty and a cavalier disregard for the cost guidelines, he estimated it could be built for £50,000.

Thomas Bellamy was another whose plans completely dominated the Square, while Karl Tottie opted for a column with a statue of Nelson reaching over 217 feet and with an internal staircase to a viewing balcony. Richard Kelsey preferred to teach a moral lesson on the subject of mercy, via a beautiful female pleading for a fallen warrior to illustrate a quote by Nelson: 'The moment an enemy submits…I become his protector'.

On 16 February 1839 the judges made their decision. Third place went to Charles Fowler and R W Sievier; second to Edward Hodges Baily, of whom more later, and the first prize was awarded to William Railton (c. 1801–1877) with his design for a tall Corinthian column supporting a statue of Nelson in his naval uniform. The column was to rise from a pediment with steps on all four sides and be guarded by huge lions couchant; the entire work would stand 203 feet tall. His subsequent estimate of the cost came to £30,500 of which £16,500 would be required for the erection of the column.

Railton was not one of the lesser known provincial architects or sculptors on whom such a prestigious commission would have conferred sudden stardom; nor was he in the same league as Chantrey, Smirke, Barry or Nash. Trained under William Inwood and at the Royal Academy Schools, he had travelled in Greece, Egypt and Corfu before setting up his practice in London. He had come fourth to Barry in the competition to design the new Houses

of Parliament. Aged about 37 at the time he won the Nelson competition, he was architect to the Ecclesiastical Commissions for whom he specialised in parsonages, and he had lately designed the Bishop of Ripon's residence. Among the country houses to his credit is the Gothic Grace-Dieu Manor in Leicestershire. From the comparatively little information that is known about him, he appears to have been a steady and reliable character, which was fortunate: the commission was going to tax his patience and determination to the limit.

Despite their choice, the judges admitted that they were concerned by the height Railton had proposed for the column, because it precluded easy recognition of the Admiral's features; the art world, led by the new *Art-Union* journal, savaged the plans, demanding a say in the judging. The final endorsement of Railton as the winner was delayed until June 1839, giving an opportunity for new entries and for changes to existing proposals, but, nevertheless, endorsed it was. However, instead of Railton being given responsibility for the whole execution, the Committee suddenly adopted the interesting idea of spreading out the contracts. Edward Hodges Baily, runner up to Railton, was commissioned to sculpt the statue of Nelson and another entrant, John Lough, was to create the four lions at the base. The sculptors of the bas relievos at the base of the column, depicting Nelson's four great battle victories, would be named at a later date.

The battle of Trafalgar Square

The location of the monument was decided upon by the Committee without reference to Railton: his drawing placed it relatively centrally; the Committee moved it to the southern edge of the Square. Despite a favourable report obtained by Railton into the load-bearing ability of the London clay, original concerns about how visible Nelson would be from 200 feet gave way to worries over the stability of what would be the world's tallest Corinthian column. The Commissioners decided to seek professional opinion. They turned to Sir Robert Smirke, the architect of the western side of the Square, and to the president of the College of Civil Engineers who reported that it would be sensible to reduce the height by 33 feet overall, 20 feet of which should be taken out of the shaft. They also recommended that the fluting of the column should be elliptical instead of semicircular, and that granite and bronze should be used for the shaft and decoration respectively. Railton acquiesced and adjusted the overall proportions of the monument, which left him with an actual shaft of 98 feet.

With Grissell and Peto engaged as contractors, work on the foundations began: hard-stock brickwork on a concrete bed, 80 feet 6 inches square, set on a layer of gravel 16 feet below the level of the Square, and this, without anyone knowing exactly what would happen to the Square itself now that Wilkins, who had put forward a proposal for its development, was dead. In April 1840, the Commissioners turned to Charles, later Sir Charles, Barry and handed him the task of laying out a rectangle with a slope, an unimposing National Gallery at one end and a very tall column about to rise up at the other.

Barry shared Wilkins' desire to level that area of the Square which was to be enclosed. From the Royal College of Physicians to Morley's Hotel the ground measured 500 feet, out of which 75 feet on either side was given over to pavements and carriageway. From the portico of the National Gallery south to the statue of Charles I it measured 470 feet. Barry proposed allocating 80 feet of this to the street in front of the Gallery, and a further 32 feet for a terrace overlooking the square. This terrace was to be 165 feet long, and at either end a flight of steps would lead into the Square. The enclosed area could, therefore, extend 350 feet east–west and, including the terrace, 290 feet north–south. The retaining walls, surmounted by a 3-foot balustrade, gradually deepened from south to north until, in front of the terrace, they reached a depth of 11 feet. The southern end was to be left open but protected from

traffic by ornamental stone posts. Barry also specified two great plinths, which might support high-quality sculpture, and pedestals for lighting. The centre of Railton's monument fell 300 feet from the National Gallery's portico. The decision to include fountains was not taken on aesthetic grounds: they were a subtle means of reducing the space for demonstrations, which were confidently expected to converge on the new open space.

Unbelievably, there was minimal liaison, either expected or actual, between Railton and Barry: it was as if their two projects were taking place on different sites. At the request of the Commissioners, Barry took his plans to Railton to check that nothing in them would cause him any problems, and that was the extent of their cooperation. Worse, not everyone shared the enthusiasm of the Nelson Memorial Committee for the project. A Select Committee was set up by Parliament, and both architects were to find themselves in front of it.

The Minutes of the Select Committee indicate that, far from being impartial, it had a hostile agenda. The members questioned Railton minutely on the changes made to his design and on the approval process. They were clearly looking for some weakness to invalidate the project, but he answered them with straight facts, whereupon they turned their attention to Alexander Milne, one of the Commissioners, again looking for flaws in the proceedings and in the accounting. Asked how much of the column had been completed, Milne informed them that he had looked in on the Square that morning, 10 July 1840, and watched the concrete pouring for the foundations.

A number of architects and sculptors, some of whom had been unsuccessful in the competition, were summoned to give their professional opinion. Asked by the Chairman if he was familiar with Barry's plans for the Square and with the Nelson monument, Sir Francis Chantrey loftily disclaimed all knowledge

Charles Barry (1795–1860), seen here in this quinessentially Victorian portrait, became one of the most sought-after architects of the period. As well as buildings, he also designed gardens, examples of which include the Italianate model of Trentham, near Stoke-on-Trent, and the Versailles-inspired Dunrobin Castle, north of Inverness, where he also remodelled the original fortress in the Scottish Baronial style.

THE LATE EDWARD HODGES BAILY, ESQ, R.A, F.R.S.

ABOVE Edward Hodges Baily (1788–1867) showed such early promise that a friend sent a piece of his work to Flaxman who took the aspirant into his studio. At 29 he was an Associate of the Royal Academy; in 1823 he sculpted Admiral St Vincent for St Paul's Cathedral. However, his portrait statues and busts won less praise than his other work.

OPPOSITE Baily at work in his studio. The picture shows both his model and the almost completed statue in two parts, and it appears that between carving the model and starting work on the full-sized version he made a slight adjustment and turned Nelson's head a little.

of either. He was handed several questions and asked to go away and think about them. Other architects were not interviewed, just given the questions. These asked for their opinion on the effect the column would have on the National Gallery; what effect the column would have as an ornamental object in that location; what effect the column would have on the gallery as approached from Whitehall; how favourable a position the site was for the column itself.

Then came Barry's turn. After describing his plans he was requested to comment on the column. He admitted he was not in favour of it: it would detract from the National Gallery. When asked to suggest a more appropriate site he came down in favour of Greenwich. If he thought he was merely there to criticise the monument, he was soon undeceived for he, too, was subjected to a close cross-examination. But as far as he was concerned, the column had been approved and that was the end of the matter.

The next victim was Charles Scott, the Secretary of the Nelson Memorial Committee, who found the Select Committee as inimical as had Railton. Again, the legality of the entire project was called into question, but Scott was able to produce a letter signed by the Chancellor of the Exchequer – though even parts of that were disputed.

The various architects returned their answers. Some, like Joseph Gwilt and Sir Richard Westmacott, were implacably opposed to the column, others, such as Sir Francis Chantrey and Thomas Donaldson clearly tried to be objective. The Select Committee recalled Railton and questioned him, this time on the circumstances surrounding his winning the competition. Then the gloves came off. Suppose the work was stopped and another competition was held, would that cause any problems? The implication was obvious. Railton hit back:

'No professional man would venture to compete again…it would be a complete breach of faith.'

'Did any first-rate artist compete last time?' demanded the Chairman.

'Several', replied Railton, who must have been indignant at such a question.

'Sir Francis Chantrey?'

'He never competes, except it is with one or two…'

The Select Committee then turned to the possibility of moving the column to Greenwich or Blackheath, to which an obviously exasperated Railton retorted that it might as well go to the Nore, and he made it obvious that he was prepared to walk away from the project if such a move went ahead.

Later, Railton dashed off a letter to the Select Committee listing the contracts entered into and the cost of the work already completed. To move the column would cost little less than £11,000. Reluctantly conceding that the Nelson Memorial Committee had been authorised to erect its monument on the site and that work had commenced, the Select Committee had to content themselves with sniping at the column and expressing grave reservations about the funding.

Those last reservations would prove to be well founded, and lack of money would not only delay completion of the monument by years but also lead to changes to Railton's design and oblige the government to make up the shortfall.

Building the Nelson monument

As Barry's groundwork began, the Square was enclosed by a large hoarding which, plastered with posters and bills, once again became a popular source of local information. Railton's memorial also began to take shape as blocks of granite from Foggin Tor in Devon were brought up the Thames. Each course of the column was made up of seven blocks: one forming part of the central core, the other six radiating out. They were held together, vertically, with slate dowels.

Of great interest to engineers was the scaffolding used for the construction. The old style of flimsy supports, based on quantity rather than quality, had been superseded by something far more substantial: heavy tiers that could be increased as required and which stood independent of the structure that was being created. The *Illustrated London News* offered this description:

> The timbers preserve the square and rugged proportions in which they floated down their native streams, and are secured to each other in the simplest and strongest manner. There are five grand uprights on standards on the east side, and a corresponding number on the west, in 6 stages or stories [*sic*] marked by the horizontal beams and curbs…the base being greatly extended and the sides strengthened by diagonal and raking braces.

A model of the scaffolding was subsequently placed in the Museum of the National Institute in New York.

The invention of steam power made raising the carefully shaped blocks of granite comparatively easy. A powerful steam engine known as a Traveller was brought in to lift the blocks. Because it ran on a short track, and because the travelling platform could be moved 90 degrees, the engine could place the blocks exactly where they were wanted.

Just as Railton must have hoped that the path of construction would now run smoothly he was hit by a labour dispute that had spilled over from Barry's Houses of Parliament, a massive project

begun in 1836. The masons there were in dispute over the bullying tactics of the foreman, and their withdrawal of labour was supported by their comrades working at Trafalgar Square. On 13 October 1840 they wrote to Grissell and Peto – who also had the construction contract for the Parliament buildings – that they would down tools at 5.30 p.m. The ensuing strike, and the attempts to break or maintain it, was costly for both employer and union. The contractors' eventual solution, rather than get rid of the foreman, was to bring in non-union labour.

The commission for the statue had gone to Edward Hodges Baily who began work almost immediately. Although Nelson had

been dead for 35 years, there was no shortage of references from which he could take a likeness. Apart from the many portraits there were a number of busts, including one in wax by Catherine Andras for whom Nelson had sat just before he left London for the last time. It was said to be so accurate that it greatly upset Emma Hamilton, Nelson's mistress, when it was shown to her. Other eminent sculptors, including Sir Francis Chantrey, John Flaxman, Franz Thaller and Matthias Ranson, jointly, and Lemuel Abbot had also produced lifelike busts, and credit has also gone to a mask of Nelson in the possession of the sculptor, John Carew. There was something appropriate in the choice of Baily for the commission: his father had been a talented carver of ships' figureheads.

Producing an image of Nelson was not as difficult as finding the stone. For safety reasons, Baily wanted to carve it out of a single block rather than assemble it from several smaller pieces. The Duke of Buccleugh came to the rescue at the end of 1840. Chairman of the Nelson Memorial Committee, he also owned a quarry near Edinburgh and was able to place a piece of Craiglieth sandstone at Baily's disposal. Almost immediately two problems arose. The stone fractured and the shipping agents felt that the transportation of any such lump of stone, weighing around 40 tons, was probably unfeasible. Questions were also being asked as to whether the technology existed to raise a one-piece statue of such weight to the top of the column. In the end, Baily was forced to compromise and his Craigleith sandstone was shipped in three pieces and set up in his studio.

A journalist from the *Illustrated London News* who saw the statue in March 1843 offered tepid praise:

It is executed by Bailey [*sic*] who has produced some
of the finest pieces of ideal sculpture the country can boast
of; it appears to us that this style of work is not suited to
him; it is a mere portrait statue, with no attempt to raise
the subject above a literal fidelity of figure and costume.

When the statue went on public display at Charing Cross shortly before it was raised, the same newspaper sang to a very different tune. It praised:

…the sharp, angular features, the expression of great activity
of mind, but of little mental grandeur; of quickness of
perception and decision; and withal that sad air, so
perceptible in the best portraits of the warrior, of long-
continued physical pain and suffering. The expression is a
peculiar one; it is more afflicting to the eyes than the
expression of deep thought; and though mournful, it is less
abstracted than that of meditation.

The writer was unhappy about the clothes, but instead of blaming Baily he complained that no artist could be expected to make nineteenth-century fashion look graceful or dignified. It was a common lament.

While the column was slowly rising and Nelson's likeness was emerging in stone, work was underway on the bronze ornamentation of the capital that would complete it. It is popularly believed that the bronze came from cannon salvaged from HMS *Royal George*, which sank with the loss of 1000 lives in 1781–2 while undergoing repairs at Portsmouth, but there is no proof. In January 1841 *The Times* reported:

The *Mary Ann* barge sailed to-day for the Tower with stores
and two 24-pounder guns raised from the wreck of the *Royal
George*. These beautiful guns are to be handed over to the
contractor to be recast in the bust of Lord Nelson, about to be
erected at Trafalgar Square.

This was a reporting error: despite some discussion about bronze in August 1839, the statue was always going to be made of stone, although critics have since complained that either it should have

been bronze from the outset or that it should be replaced with bronze. None of this rules out the cannons of the *Royal George* being used for the capital: it is far too attractive a legend to be dismissed for lack of evidence.

Wherever it came from, the bronze would be cast at Woolwich to form the massive volutes and acanthus leaves – some weighing over 2 tons – based on the example of Mars Ultor in Rome.

Misfortune dogged the casting of the ornaments, with the death of the first contractor forcing Railton to find a second. Work on the column had to be halted for nine months while the bronzes were being produced, and on one occasion the back of the furnace collapsed, spilling more than 700 pounds of molten metal into the coals. Site work resumed towards the end of July 1843 when the first castings were lifted into position and fixed to the capital by means of huge hooks, eyes and rivets. It would take until the very end of August to complete that task, and Railton was hoping that the statue would be raised on 21 October – Trafalgar Day.

Before that, the scaffolding had to be raised yet another level and the Traveller steam engine would haul up another few tons of Craigleith stone representing the plinth, or tambour, on which the statue would stand. Without this plinth to elevate him, the lower half of Nelson would have been obscured by the wide capital. It is said that shortly before Nelson took possession of his column a group of workers celebrated their achievements with a beefsteak dinner on the very top.

Trafalgar Day came, and went; not until 3 November was Nelson ready to begin the ascent.

The engineers could hardly have slept the night before as they made sure that the engine's boiler was up to pressure ready for the early morning hoist. Final adjustments to the lower half of the statue were made at 5.20 a.m., and the order was given to commence raising it. The movement was hardly perceptible. Nelson's legs reached the first stage at 6.45, the second at 8.08, the third at 9.25, the fourth at 10.23 and the top at 11.20. At 11.45

the lower block was in position. One can only imagine the tension and the relief. It is hardly surprising that Railton waited until the following day to hoist the second and lighter block, fixing it into place with dowels of York stone, 10 inches square and 1 foot 9 inches long.

Public reaction was, as expected, divided. A less than complimentary article in the *Examiner*, January 1844, purported to quote an old sailor as saying: 'My eyes…they've mast-headed the Admiral!' Being sent to the top of the mast was a common punishment for an errant a midshipman, and the article laboured the theme:

> The mast is sufficiently represented by the column, and the capital of it is in the closest resemblance to the cross-trees… [It] is much the same thing as putting a grown gentleman into the corner with a fool's cap on his head.

Another complaint was against the coil of rope behind Nelson's feet, essential to give the figure stability. Nobody, however, was more vitriolic than a later French visitor, Hippolyte Taine, who in 1852 likened Nelson on his column to a rat impaled on a pole.

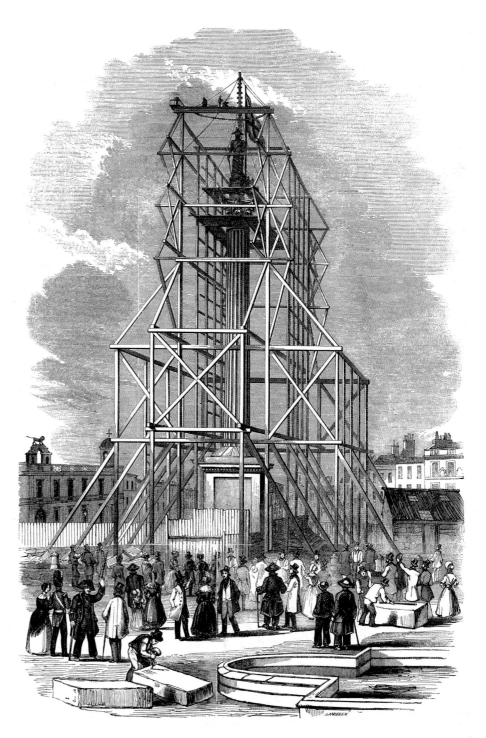

On 4 November 1843 Nelson finally stared out over the capital city that had been so slow to honour his sacrifice. The ensign flying above him was a real flag, put up for the occasion, not part of the sculpture. In the foreground, a mason works on the fountain basin.

CHAPTER 3 LAYING CLAIM TO THE SQUARE

The Square is opened

By the end of 1843 Charles Barry's structural work in the Square was nearing completion. The terrace was paved with red and white Mansfield stone from Nottinghamshire, placed lozenge fashion, with bands of Portland and York stone, an early contract for the embryonic Mowlem construction company. Aberdeen granite was used for the balustrading and bollards, and soon the Bastienne Bitumen Company would cover some 37,000 square feet with asphalt, inlaid by Messrs Maude with Portland stone bands and a white star. This asphalt was never popular and was replaced later in the century with paving slabs. The two great plinths at the

north side were in position and at the end of November an equestrian statue of George IV, 13 feet high and weighing 7 tons, materialised without warning on the pedestal nearest St Martin-in-the-Fields, where it can been seen today. It was the work of Sir Francis Chantrey (1782–1841), commenced in 1829 but not completed until much later. Originally it had been commissioned for the Marble Arch, but this plan changed with the King's death. Chantrey, by then one of the most respected and highly paid of his profession, was instructed to continue with it, which he did; slowly. It had not long been completed when he died – it was still in his studio – and a home was found for it in Trafalgar Square, one intended to be temporary.

Chantrey's depiction of George IV was generally agreed to be a good likeness, although it reduced the Monarch's corpulence. For the first time in such sculpture the horse had all four feet on the

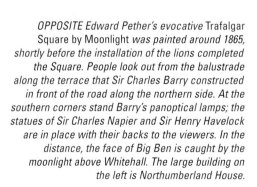

OPPOSITE Edward Pether's evocative Trafalgar Square by Moonlight *was painted around 1865, shortly before the installation of the lions completed the Square. People look out from the balustrade along the terrace that Sir Charles Barry constructed in front of the road along the northern side. At the southern corners stand Barry's panoptical lamps; the statues of Sir Charles Napier and Sir Henry Havelock are in place with their backs to the viewers. In the distance, the face of Big Ben is caught by the moonlight above Whitehall. The large building on the left is Northumberland House.*

RIGHT Sir Francis Chantrey's statue of George IV stood 'temporarily' at Trafalgar Square for more than half a century before the plinth was engraved with the Monarch's name – and then only after someone demanded to know whom the statue represented.

ground, of which one critic said, 'the change is for the better'. By contrast, the *Examiner*, having savaged Baily's Nelson, turned with even more gleeful venom on George IV: 'The king…looks marvellously ill at ease and imbecile with his legs dangling down. In his right hand he holds a roll of bills (marking the time when he was Prince Regent)'.

Given the prevailing artistic wisdom that contemporary fashion could never achieve the dignity of the Roman toga or Greek himation, Chantrey's 'conventional compromise between modern and classic costume', as the *Illustrated London News* described it, failed to impress *Punch*: 'Posterity will be under the impression that George IV used to ride about…with a tremendous quantity of table linen suspended from his shoulders'.

As Barry pushed for a completion date of 1 May 1844, lack of funds left work on Railton's Column suspended. The prospect of the Square opening while the monument was unfinished brought an understandable blast from *The Times* at the end of April. Sarcastically commenting that when the main hoarding came down the people of London would still be able to post their bills and stickers on the smaller hoarding around the base of the Column, the writer fulminated:

The column that has been placed in Trafalgar Square to Trafalgar's hero cannot be finished for want of funds; and thus is everything in this country done; we never complete anything properly in the first instance, and doubtless £10,000 must be voted to erect the steps and place the lions at the base of the column at the public expense.

This early 1850s view from the south-west, showing the Square after Barry levelled it, illustrates the pronounced slope of the site. The creation of the north wall and terrace with steps down on either side elevates the National Gallery, while the laying out of the roads and pavements begins to turn the Square into a huge roundabout.

The Globe called the problem, 'a stigma on our national character. We still hope that the government will come forwards and…prevent what should be a national monument becoming a national disgrace'.

The great hoarding was removed and on 2 May the public had their first full view of the still incomplete Square. The fountain basins were built but the fountains themselves were not yet ready. It was something of a disappointment, as was the behaviour of those who visited the latest attraction in the city. Within a couple of days of the opening there were complaints that, instead of using the inadequate public toilet behind the National Gallery, people were urinating at will in the Square and children were throwing all manner of things from orange peel to rags and paper into the fountains. An incensed letter-writer to *The Times* castigated the police for either standing around doing nothing or else eyeing up the women instead of doing the duty for which they were very well paid.

Fountains and light in the Square

Work to supply the fountains was in hand. In the summer of 1843 the Southwark engineering company Messrs Easton and Amos had recommended the use of artesian wells, adding that they believed these wells could also supply all the government departments in the area and the new Houses of Parliament. This was music to the ears of the Commissioners of HM Woods, Forests and Land Revenues, who had already decided that it would be too expensive

BELOW LEFT Barry's fountains were carved from very hard red granite from the Aberdeen area, which could be highly polished. It was praised for its durability, allowing one humorist to express the view that while the granite was durable, the fountains themselves were unendurable.

BELOW RIGHT The steam engine for the fountains. The engraving shows the great beam on its pivot. At the far left it is attached to the piston; on the right, rods A and B are attached to the pumps. Pump A sends water to the government offices; the larger Pump B can raise up to 800 gallons per minute for the fountains. C is the small direct-acting engine usually in reserve.

The fountains may have disappointed the adults, but on a warm day they provided only fascination for younger visitors, a welcome relief from the overwhelming architecture and endless pavements of the capital.

to use the public water companies for the fountains. They calculated that by switching to artesian wells they could supply more offices for the same cost and actually run the fountains, which would be pumping 300,000 gallons of water a day, for nothing.

The water to supply these wells lay about 250 feet from the surface in a deep layer of green sand and chalk. Rainfall on the chalk hills of the Downs and the Chilterns percolates through the porous rock and, sandwiched between impermeable strata, gathers under pressure beneath London. When a borehole is drilled through the thick clay, that pressure forces the water to rise up to the surface. In the case of London, so many boreholes had been sunk that the water would only rise to 100 feet or so below the surface, requiring a steam-powered pumping engine to abstract it.

Easton and Amos secured a site in Orange Street behind the National Gallery for their engine house and set to work drilling two artesian wells. The first was at Orange Street itself where the ground was 42 feet above Trinity High Water Mark.

Here, to a depth of 174 feet, they drilled a wide shaft, at first oval then circular with a diameter of some 6 feet, through the earth, gravel and a thick stratum of London clay. From this point a smaller pipe of 15-inch diameter was sunk through a layer of plastic clay and into a stratum of gravel, sand and stones. Finally a 7-inch diameter pipe went down through green sand and into the chalk, taking the well to 300 feet through a few million years of geological history.

The second, narrower well, 400 feet to the south and so situated in front of the National Gallery, commenced at 29 feet above Trinity High Water Mark, reflecting the gradient of the valley of the Thames, and went down a total of 395 feet.

The two wells were linked by a horizontal tunnel, 6 feet in diameter. The digging of this tunnel was a dangerous business; water burst in while it was under construction, almost drowning the workers. Smaller pipes were also laid, connecting Orange Street and the fountains.

The engineers needed water to prevent the great Cornish pumping engine from overheating, but could not abstract the extra volume from the wells. The alternative was to create large cooling ponds. Their ingenious solution was to use the fountain basins. A second, smaller engine ensured circulation round the basins, and was also available if the Cornish engine was shut down for maintenance. Each engine was fitted with a Jackson's patent smoke-consuming furnace so no ugly plumes of smoke rose over the National Gallery to spoil the effect.

Steam power had made possible the Industrial Revolution, and technology was a source of fascination to the Victorians. Both engines, like the Orange Street works, are long gone, but the Kew Bridge Steam Museum has some splendid examples of Cornish pumping engines still in steam, and an Easton and Amos pumping engine of a different design.

Barry had designed the fountains as well as the basins in which they stood but they never found popular favour and were replaced a century later. The problem lay not just with the artistic design but also with the water supply. Barry intended each fountain to run at 500 gallons per minute and be able to throw up 1000 if required for a special occasion. In the event, that was asking too much of the artesian wells. Nevertheless, the government was content. The project came in at less than £10,000 and with running costs of £500 a year, around half the current payment to the water companies, it would pay for itself in less than 20 years. As early as March 1846 a new pump was installed to supply an additional 250 gallons per minute and this enabled the laying of a water main to both Buckingham Palace and St James's Palace as well as a contract to provide water in all the streets of St Martin's Parish.

Barely two months after the fountains had begun to play in Trafalgar Square, it was suddenly noticed, in June 1844, that Lord Nelson was showing a slight list. This appears to have been an illusion, easily corrected by a reduction of the sculpted cable supporting the figure.

Cleanliness and antisocial behaviour now became a problem. When workmen were sent to clean the basins in 1854 the ankle-deep filth, so putrid that it kept visitors at a healthy distance, included the decomposing remains of cats and dogs. (In more recent times, cleaners have removed stockings, pistols, a stuffed pike and foreign coins.) Graffiti appeared remarkably quickly. In May 1845 police ordered a man to stop chalking 'Napoleon for ever' on the pavement between the fountains. When he refused, they attempted to arrest him, whereupon he hurled himself into the fountain basin in an apparent attempt to drown himself. The water was too shallow but he may have hit his head on the stonework because he had to be taken away by stretcher. The following year, 1846, a letter published in *The Times* observed:

It is six months since four very magnificent gas lamps were erected at the public expense in Trafalgar Square and everyone…rejoiced then in the prospect of an abatement of a palpable and disgusting nuisance. If those lamps had only been lighted as well as erected, there must necessarily have been an end to the nightly practises to which I need not more particularly allude.

The 'very magnificent gas lamps' to which the letter-writer alluded had been installed in 1845, designed by Barry and manufactured by Messrs Stevens and Co. at Southwark. The framework of the panoptical lantern was cast from heavy gunmetal and the bevelled glass, an inch thick, was cut to provide the maximum refraction.

Barry had settled on the Bude method of lighting, by which a stream of oxygen is passed through the flame of an oil or spirit lamp. The technique was named after the Cornish town where the surgeon-turned-inventor, Sir Goldsworthy Gurney, had built a house. His inventions include a steam carriage that could run on the public road, the high-pressure steam jet, and a blow torch. His Bude Light was installed in the Houses of Parliament and also in

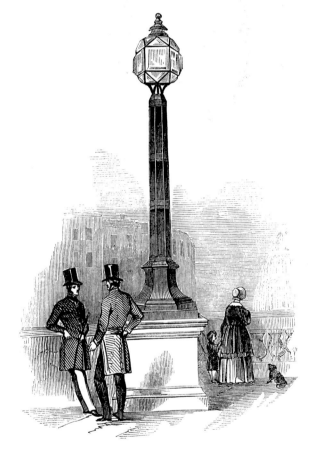

The story that the panoptical lamps came from HMS Victory *has proved remarkably enduring. In fact, Barry designed them himself. The two on the terrace were set up on tall columns; the pair at the south, on cylindrical granite drums.*

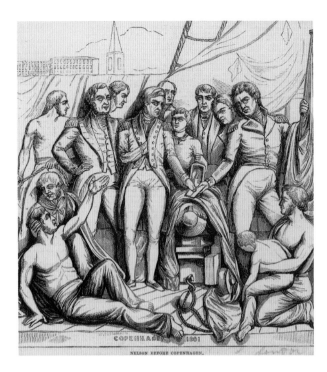

Engraving of the sculpture showing the bombardment of Copenhagen by John Ternouth. John Timbs describes it in his Curiosities of London, 1867: *'Nelson is sealing, on the end of a gun, his despatch to send by the flag of truce; a group of officers surround him, and a sailor holds a candle and lantern: in the foreground are wounded groups; and in the distance are a church and city (Copenhagen) in flames'.*

theatres where it replaced limelight. It was not a success in Trafalgar Square and was soon replaced.

Hardly had gas lighting been installed than the Square was the venue for a demonstration of scientific and technological advance that must have shaken the crowd of spectators. In 1848 Edward Staite showed off the potential of his invention: the electric arc light. Although his was not the first public display of the new technology it was, to judge from the vivid report in the *Patent Journal and Inventors' Magazine*, the most exciting. Staite had set up his apparatus so that it could:

> …illuminate the whole of Trafalgar Square, the rays reaching up as far as Northumberland House… The rays were continually moved, and as they swept through the foggy atmosphere they produced the same sort of illumination as the sunlight through atoms of dust. The objects upon which they fell were most brilliantly lighted. Nelson's column…being frequently as conspicuous as noonday.

The writer ended prophetically: 'If the illumination can be sustained, there is no other means of lighting the streets which can at all be compared with this electric light'. Unfortunately for Staite, he could not get the backing for such an expensive process and his company failed shortly after. With one small exception, Trafalgar Square remained lit by gas for another century.

Completing the Nelson monument

The Nelson Memorial Committee, meanwhile, had already faced up to the fact that they would never find the money to complete the Column. They were forced – as the Select Committee had feared – to go cap in hand to the Treasury. At their final meeting on 20 July 1844 they reported that the Lords of the Treasury believed the monument ought to be finished and would recommend the same. Moneys and plans would be handed over,

and after thanking Charles Scott for his work as Secretary, the Committee, as the minutes put it, 'separated'.

Lord Lincoln was the man now in charge of the Commissioners of HM Woods, Forests and Land Revenues, though only for another three years, and he was determined to save money. He immediately scrapped the steps that Railton had intended to lead spectators up to the base of the column, but eventually the bas relievos went ahead – albeit with changes to three of the four sculptors who had originally been sought for the work. Railton had already specified the four battles he wished to see commemorated – St Vincent, the Nile, Copenhagen and Trafalgar – and having shared them out between themselves, the four sculptors commenced work in 1847. The bas relievos were to be approximately 14 feet square so that the main figures could be portrayed not less than 6 feet high. The depth was to be no more than 15 inches.

Born at Dalston Hall near Carlisle, Musgrave Lewthwaite Watson (1804–1847) had trained as a solicitor before changing career and studying art at the Royal Academy Schools. Times had changed since James Gibbs had become the first British architect to be trained abroad, and Watson went to Rome to continue his study. Aged 24 he returned to England where he worked under both Sir Francis Chantrey and Edward Baily before setting up his own studio around 1842. Considered to be a man of volatile temperament, he also had scant regard for the conventions of the age, cohabiting with the daughter of a pub landlord from Carlisle. His Battle of Cape St Vincent for the Nelson monument is his most famous work and he might well have become one of the finest sculptors of his day if his life had not been cut short by a fatal heart condition. He did not even live to see his bronze relief completed, cast and set in place on the west side facing the Union Club.

The Battle of the Nile was in the hands of William Frederick Woodington (1806–1893), the most famous sculptor of the quartet.

Born in Sutton Coldfield, he grew up in London and began his career as an engraver before emulating his master, R W Sievier, in changing to sculpture. He was beginning to make a name for himself: his *Milton Dictating to his Daughter* and *The Deluge* both getting excellent reviews. He then went on to produce two portraits for the House of Lords before working on the Nelson bas relief for which he, like Watson, is best remembered. During his long career he exhibited at the Royal Academy until 1882, dying at the end of 1893. He took over Watson's incomplete work, and

when his sculpture was put into place it was erroneously reported in the press that both he and Watson were dead – a mistake that he felt impelled to correct.

John Ternouth (1795–1849) found himself trying to make something dramatic out of the Battle of Copenhagen, which was fought to end the Armed Neutrality Alliance of Sweden, Russia and Denmark. Ternouth was not a brilliant sculptor, but he was a regular exhibitor at the Royal Academy. Towards the end of his career his output was so small that he was believed dead. On 14

The bas relief of the Battle of the Nile by William Frederick Woodington. John Timbs describes the moment Nelson is wounded in his Curiosities of London, 1867: *'And Nelson, having received a severe wound in the head, was caught by Captain Berry in his arms, as he was falling, and carried into the cockpit; the surgeon is quitting a wounded sailor that he may instantly attend the Admiral. "No", said Nelson; "I will take my turn with my brave fellows."'*

The magnitude of the commission to sculpt the four lions, which would complete the Nelson monument, weighed on Edwin Landseer (1802–73). During the 1860s his letters regularly alluded to 'lionizing' and a sketch owned by the Marquis of Salisbury, captioned 'My last night's nightmare', depicts him lying on the ground with a huge lion over him. Its mouth is open and it rests its huge forelegs on him.

November 1846 the *Athenæum* printed: 'Mr Ternouth has written to say he is not dead and we give him the benefit of the doubt'.

John Edward Carew (1785–1868), the oldest and arguably the most experienced of the quartet took on the most high profile of the bronzes, Trafalgar, and unsurprisingly chose to portray the death of Nelson. In 1809, aged about 24, the Dublin-trained sculptor had come to London to work for Sir Richard Westmacott where, by his own account, he earned a small fortune. Then, from 1822 until 1837 he worked exclusively for the Earl of Egremont and his work can be seen at Petworth. The financial arrangements were somewhat loose: instead of specific payments for particular commissions, Carew received very generous ad hoc sums of money and gained the impression that he would inherit under the Earl's will. Disappointed in his expectations, he made a claim for an incredible £50,000, which the executors decided to take to court, paying Carew's expenses so that the matter could be decided openly. The loss of the case bankrupted him but he continued his career until partially blind. He died in November 1868, his reputation as an artist assured.

The sculptors were to be paid £1000 each, which had to include the cost of casting their designs in bronze but not the cost of the bronze itself. This was to be supplied by the government so that there would be no cutting corners by making thin reliefs that might buckle or be easily dented. Any unused bronze was to be returned, so, again, there would be no incentive for fraud. Or so the Commissioners fondly believed.

There was no grand ceremony to celebrate the placing in position of the four huge sculptures. Once again delays, caused this time by the Commissioners, by the death of Watson and by Woodington's ill health, robbed the project of its lustre. Each panel was erected when it was ready. First to appear was Carew's Trafalgar, all 5 tons of it, in December 1849. The cast had absorbed the bronze from five melted down mortars and one 32-pound cannon (the weight referring to the weight of the shot that the cannon could fire). It had been cast in three sections by Adams, Christie and Company who had set up the mould in a vertical rather than horizontal position, which gave a finer surface finish. The cost, however, was almost twice the tender. There was some concern that the panel was not entirely square, but the inaccuracy was minimal and no action was taken, particularly because the foundry was going through bankruptcy proceedings.

Woodington's Nile, cast by Moore, Fressange and Moore was put up in March of the following year, weighing 2 tons 15 cwt. Later, in the summer of 1852 two workers from the foundry tipped off the Commissioners that their company had committed fraud over the two casts it had made for Woodington. Not only had the bronze been adulterated with cast iron and plaster but that false weights had been used when the final weighing took place. This meant that the foundry had been able to hold back a considerable quantity of the bronze for itself. The matter ended in court and all three partners went to prison for between one and three months. It also meant finding a new foundry for Watson/ Woodington's Cape St Vincent, which was not installed until 1854. In the meantime, Ternouth's Copenhagen was put up early in January 1851.

For Railton, whatever pleasure and pride he had taken in winning the Nelson Monument Commission must have evaporated years earlier, replaced by frustration and a weary desire to see the project finished. He had experienced nothing but interference, insult and delay in a project that was supposed to glorify Nelson and all he stood for, but which had descended into either farce or tragedy. And he was still short of his four lions.

The lions

John Lough, the original sculptor charged with the commission for the lions, had wisely washed his hands of the affair in 1846. He had been given a budget of £3000 for four 25-foot lions but immediately complained that he could not do them for less than 3000 guineas even if they were only 20 feet long. If the Committee insisted on 25-foot lions, they were looking at 4000 guineas as each sculpture would need 141 tons of granite. After six years of delays, he withdrew.

His replacement, Thomas Milnes, produced four stone lions with the names War, Peace, Vigilance and Determination, but they were rejected. Legend has it that they were based on the domestic cat, and the way that Peace licks its front paw certainly suggests lazy contentment rather than the kind of peace won with blood and cannonballs. Returned to their creator, they can be seen today at Saltaire, near Bradford.

In 1858 the Commissioners abruptly turned to the painter, Sir Edwin Landseer, and offered him the commission. It was a decision that provoked open-mouthed astonishment and ended as a national embarrassment. It was not just that Landseer had never sculpted anything before, but that he was well known for getting behind with commissions. The handsome raconteur, who had been drawing animals since the age of 4, who had exhibited at the Royal Academy at the age of 13, and who became a Royal Academician before he was 30, had suffered a mental breakdown in 1843 and he never recovered from it. He became unreliable, difficult and sometimes offensive to clients – even those as important at Queen Victoria, who knighted him in 1850. The damage to his career might have been even greater but for the loyalty of his business manager and friend, Jacob Bell, who stood between him and his dissatisfied customers.

Yet although he procrastinated over this commission, he was determined upon zoological accuracy. When one of London Zoo's lions died, the corpse was sent to him. The servant who opened the door is said to have gone to his master and asked, much as he might have enquired if Landseer had sent out for a pizza, 'Did you order a lion, Sir Hedwin [sic]?' Landseer had also asked for casts of a statue of a lion in Turin – casts, because the animal had been in pieces following dissection – and these were duly provided.

Artistic delay was not the only cause for concern: the costs had multiplied wildly since Railton's original figure of £3000. The lions were cast at the foundry of Baron Marochetti, an Italian-born

but French-naturalised sculptor famous for equestrian statues, and who had left France in the wake of the 1848 revolution that had finally established France as a republic. Marochetti charged close to £11,000 for materials and labour; a home-grown foundry allegedly claimed they could do it for £6000. Landseer's own fee was £6000. Furthermore, there was genuine concern regarding the quality of the casting.

The lions were unveiled to the public at the very beginning of February 1867 in an extremely low-key ceremony from which Railton, now long retired, was absent. Landseer, Marochetti and some of the senior officials at the Office of Works – which had succeeded the Commissioners of HM Woods, Forests and Land Revenues – were there to see the canvas shrouds removed and

Landseer captured the majesty of the lions if not their exact shape. Critics pointed out that his lions had concave rather than the rounded backs that lions exhibit when lying down. Their architectural relationship with the column was weakened by the scrapping of Railton's original plan to separate them with flights of steps.

the final pieces of the Nelson monument revealed to the public, 41 years after the man they were honouring had died. A clear leader who told his captains the plan of battle and expected them to use their experience and initiative to see it through, Nelson would have been astonished at the controversy, inefficiency, fraud and incompetence that had delayed his monument and pushed the costs towards that originally voted to build the National Gallery.

The first protests

It is probably sensible at this moment to step back to the laying out of the Square. From that period onwards, the story is not solely about the built environment but encompasses the events that were played out within the Square's boundaries or reflected in its changes. It was a large open space, centrally located within a city that the railways were rapidly making far more accessible; a place where ordinary people could congregate in large numbers.

Already it had become one of the sites from which to view the monarch. The Victorians were not bombarded with media images as we are. The *Illustrated London News* and, later, the *Lady's Newspaper* carried engravings, but in reality anyone in London who wished to see their new queen had either to look in their pocket for a coin, or stand along the processional route, which they did in their thousands.

Where people could gather to celebrate, they could also come to demonstrate, and this was an age of protest. There was, after all, a great deal to protest about. In 1836 The London Working Men's Association had joined with a group of radical MPs to urge a number of important reforms, and, leaving areas of disagreement to one side, they had set out their common aims in a six-point charter:

1. A vote for every man twenty-one years of age, of sound mind, and not undergoing punishment for crime.
2. The secret ballot.
3. No property qualification for Members of Parliament.
4. Payment of Members.
5. Equal constituencies.
6. Annual parliaments.

The crowds turned out in their thousands for the coronation of Queen Victoria in 1838. In this scene from a contemporary panorama, the carriage of Count Guglielmo de Ludolf, the Ambassador for Sicily, passes the statue of Charles I.

Effendi. *Resident Ambassadors.* *Sicillian.* *Count Ludolf.* *Belgian.*

From this came the name Chartists, and branches of the organisation sprang up in various towns and cities, urging reform through peaceful protest. In 1837 they presented a moving and well-argued petition to Parliament calling for a fairer society to unite rather than divide the classes. It was not, however, a call to which the government was prepared to listen at that time. The Congress of Vienna, which had settled the map of Europe after the Napoleonic Wars, had attempted to restore much of the pre-1792 status quo across Europe. But there were revolts in Europe during 1830, and more in 1848. Fears of a French-style revolution in Great Britain made the Establishment as a whole very nervous and the flight of King Louis Philippe early in 1848 gave heart not just to the Chartists but to those who felt that only violent action would improve their lot. There were disturbances and riots across the country.

A protest against Income Tax (a burden that had originally been imposed to raise money for the Napoleonic Wars but which successive governments found too lucrative to abolish) scheduled for 6 March 1848 in Trafalgar Square was banned by the police, because it would be taking place within a mile of Westminster Hall while Parliament was sitting. The organisers posted notices of the cancellation on the day itself advising protestors to go home, but several thousand assembled, turning the demonstration into a Chartist rally in support of the French republicans and an advertisement for a much larger event to follow at Kennington. At the height of the protest an estimated 15,000 people were in Trafalgar Square and it eventually took 500 police to restore order. The *Lady's Newspaper* printed an amusing account of the protest which, while large and passionate, hardly smacked of bloody and violent revolution:

When the speechifying, such as it was, had ceased, it was expected that the vast concourse of the people…would quietly disperse; but the mischievous tendencies of the mob

Queen Victoria, seen here in 1849 with Prince Albert and three of their children, made a point of visiting the Royal Academy every year before its annual exhibition opened to the public. The natural light from the lantern roof is supplemented by candles.

PASSING TRAFALGAR SQUARE.

LONDON, PUB. BY MACLURE, MACDONALD & MACGREGOR
LITHOG.RS TO THE QUEEN

returned, and unluckily the small body of policemen scattered about the square became the object of persecution. No sooner was one of these found alone, than a ring was formed around him, and, unless he produced his truncheon without delay, his hat was thrust over his eyes, and thus 'bonneted', as the term goes, he was hustled and twirled about in every direction of the crowd.

The subsequent great rally at Kennington, south London, peaceful as it was, proved the beginning of the end. An old law was invoked which prohibited the handing in of petitions by groups greater than ten; many thousands of police, Special Constables and members of the armed forces guarded the capital; and the 5,700,000 signatures that the organisers claimed for their petition was swiftly denounced by the government to be a massive overstatement; indeed, several of the names, including 'Victoria Rex', 'Flatnose' and the 'Duke of Wellington', were highly suspect. The year 1848 turned out to be the last year in which the Chartist cause would claim massive national support.

The Trafalgar Square demonstration had set something of a precedent: Charles Barry may have thought he had given the country its seat of government in the shape of his magnificent gothic building by the Thames at Westminster, but in fact it was his less ostentatious Italianate open space that would become, in the words of a future statesman, 'the real parliament of the country'. The descendants of those who had covered Daniel Defoe's pillory in flowers to send a message to the government would from now on congregate in Trafalgar Square to voice their grievances.

Not all the events that took place in the Square were on such a large scale; some were private tragedies such as that of elderly Caroline Pultney in March 1845, a poverty-stricken needlewoman clearly suffering a breakdown, who attempted to commit suicide in one of the fountain basins. Taken to the police station she even tried to strangle herself. On another occasion, in May 1850, a young man by the name of George Longfellow was heard shouting for help from the fountains. Those who went to his aid found him holding up the unconscious body of a woman. He and his wife had seen her hurl herself headfirst into the water and assumed she, too, was trying to kill herself. She was taken to Charing Cross Hospital where, on regaining consciousness, she gave her name as Katherine Morris and informed the doctors that she had been baptising herself. But from other disjointed sentences she uttered it was obvious that she, too, was in need of the kind of help that Victorian Britain just did not offer. The reporting of such stories was not followed by editorials demanding that something be done; they were entertainment for much of the readership.

Wellington's funeral

If people could gather to celebrate and protest, they could also gather to mourn. On 14 September 1852 the Duke of Wellington died. Almost half a century elapsed between the deaths of Britain's two great heroes of the Napoleonic Wars. Nelson fell in battle in 1805; the Duke of Wellington went on from his 'near run thing' at Waterloo to become Prime Minister and to die in his bed. He had not been a popular politician, regarded as too reactionary and, as a result of his military career, autocratic: 'I gave them their orders and they wanted to stay and discuss them', was his comment on his very first Cabinet meeting. All that was forgotten at his death.

The funeral, which had required weeks of planning, was a grand occasion, and arguably the most impressive since Nelson's. The houses along the route from Horse Guards to St Paul's Cathedral, passing Trafalgar Square, were hung with black and crowded with people, some on the roofs and some on specially erected scaffolding. Wellington's coffin was carried on a

…gigantic funeral car…the lions' heads projecting from the bosses of the wheels, the gracefully conventionalised figures

OPPOSITE One of the most moving moments during the funeral of the Duke of Wellington occurred when the procession passed Trafalgar Square and it was joined by veterans of his army from the Chelsea Hospital. On a tragic note, one of the many rooftop spectators slipped and fell to his death from Drummond's Bank.

Napier's portrait, like his statue, depicts him as well groomed – the epitome of the Victorian officer. His statue purports to show him at the annexation of Scinde. However, on the occasion he apparently wore an old jacket, grubby white trousers without braces and a peaked cap. His nose was so hooked his regiment called him Old Fagin and his thick beard reached his chest.

of Victory which fill the intervals between the flanges, the magnificent dolphins…wrought out along the spokes, and the relievos of the sword sheathed in laurel…the magnificent casting of the Duke's arms in bronze…the sumptuous pall, powdered with silver embroidery…and the no less superb canopy of silver tissue…

Representatives of the nobility, the army, the navy, the government, the judiciary and the City were out in force; famous regiments including the Rifles, the Scots Greys and the Duke's 'own' 33rd helped form the procession; many European nations sent their generals to pay their respects. Accompanied by her children, Queen Victoria watched the cortege pass Buckingham Palace.

The statue of Sir Charles Napier

One of the pallbearers at Wellington's funeral was himself to die the following year, inspiring an outpouring of public affection and a statue in Trafalgar Square. Son of an army officer, Charles Napier (1782–1853) had been one of Wellington's dashing young officers out in the Peninsula, but terribly wounded at Corruna in 1806, he became a prisoner of the French. To their unstinting medical care he owed his life; yet after being released in 1810 he went back into action only to be shot in the face. His military career was never less than eventful, but he spent the 1820s as Resident (a type of governor) of Cephalonia, the Greek island more recently made famous by *Captain Corelli's Mandolin*, setting in train many public works including building the island's road system. While there he met the poet, Lord Byron, who was greatly impressed by him and thought him the ideal man to serve the cause of Greek independence to which he himself was committed.

After a short break in service Napier became commander of troops in the north of England at the time of the Chartist movement – an organisation with whose aims he sympathised. On 12 January 1840 he wrote in his diary:

Patrolled all last night. Saw the Chartist sentinels in the streets; we knew they were armed with pistols, but I advised the magistrates not to meddle with them. Seizing these men could do no good; it would not stop Chartism if they were all hanged; and as they offered no violence, why starve their wretched families and worry them with a long imprisonment? I repeat it, Chartism cannot be stopped. God forbid that it should: what we want is to stop the letting loose of a large body of armed cut-throats upon the public.

While deploring the violence and putting it down, he also castigated the cruel Poor Law which drove people to it: 'The hatred to this law is not confined to Chartists, nor to the poor, it creates Chartists, it makes them sanguinary…in short it is all hell, or likely to be so in England'.

The following year he was sent to India where, during the Afghan War, he had the task of holding the line in the north-west frontier. His three victories led to the controversial annexation of the province of Scinde. He is believed to have announced his success in a punning one-word telegram: '*Peccavi*' (Latin for I have sinned). This, however, may be a myth, prompted by a letter to the satirical magazine *Punch* suggesting *peccavi* as an erudite pun on the capture of the province.

By the standards of his day, he attempted to be a good governor, one of his reforms being the outlawing of suttee: 'You say that it is your custom to burn widows. Very well. We also have a custom: when men burn a woman alive, we tie a rope around their necks and we hang them… You may follow your customs, and then we will follow ours.' A soldier much loved by the men he commanded, he resigned on principle when the wages paid to the Indian regiments under his command were reduced on the grounds that now Scinde was British they no longer qualified for the additional payments to soldiers serving 'abroad'. He died on 29 August 1853 and his funeral took place a few days later at

Portsmouth where the population filled the streets to watch the cortege. Many of the 2500 or more ordinary soldiers, 'those much-abused and reviled privates' as he once called them, who lined the route or came to pay their respects, had travelled at their own expense from Gosport and beyond.

The morning of 20 November 1856 was foul: the sky grey with sleet, the ground cold and slushy. A group of hardy souls braved the elements to watch as Napier's statue, erected on a pedestal at the south-west corner of Trafalgar Square, was quietly unveiled. Workmen climbed their ladders and carefully drew back the canvas sheet that had hidden the bronze figure since its erection after dark a couple of days previously. In addition to the man's name and dates, the inscription on the plinth recorded: 'Erected by public subscription from all classes, civil and military, the most numerous subscribers being public soldiers'. The *Art Journal* called the statue by George Adams (1821–1898), 'perhaps the worst piece of sculpture in England', because Adams had been constrained into producing an idealistic rather than a realistic likeness.

War, mutiny and General Havelock

In the same year Napier died, Britain was on the verge of yet another war, this time in the Crimea, the Russian peninsula that eats into the northern waters of the Black Sea. The Guards were waved off from Trafalgar Square by great crowds who could have no idea of the hell into which the men were going: ill-equipped for the Russian winter, poorly supplied, and with little more medical help than Florence Nightingale's small band was able to offer. The British alone lost some 22,000 men, four fifths of them to disease, and around 13,000 were wounded.

After the fall of Sebastopol in 1855 peace was made; and two years later British minds were turned towards another conflict, this time in India where Indian troops formerly loyal to the British had mutinied in large numbers. The next statue to be raised in the Square would be that of a man who died during that war.

Once again, the causes are far from simple. When the British dismissed local rulers or ended the right of succession, it mattered less that those rulers were not popular than that Indian society and religion felt itself even further under attack; decisions such as that over which Napier had resigned again gave justified grievance; and the annexation of states caused anger. But the single event that sparked the Mutiny was the issuing of the Enfield 55 rifle to the troops. A rumour went round that the bullets were greased either with cow or pig fat. Hindus regard the cow as sacred; Muslims consider the pig unclean. This was the final insult. The Mutiny was to be a bloody affair with horrific atrocities on both sides.

At the outbreak of war, Henry Havelock (1795–1857) had spent 32 years as a soldier in India, although he had never planned on a military life. After his father lost his fortune he had begun training as a solicitor, but after he quarrelled with his father he had to look for a new career. A deeply religious man, a fluent speaker of Persian and Hindi, and a staunch disciplinarian, he was personally courageous and a good tactician. During the Mutiny he was sent with 1000 troops to support the British garrisons at Cawnpore and Lucknow. Before he could reach the first, he learned of the massacre of the garrison on 3 July 1857 but he continued, hoping in vain to save the women and children. From Cawnpore, he pushed on to Lucknow with Sir James Outram who, despite having just been appointed superior to Havelock, generously allowed the friend he respected to maintain command of the operation. They successfully fought their way to the Residence at Lucknow, which they decided to hold while waiting for reinforcements. Sir Colin Campbell duly arrived bringing with him news of Havelock's knighthood, but there was little time to enjoy the honour: Havelock had contracted dysentery and died eight days later on 24 November 1857 in the arms of his wounded son.

Early in 1858 the government offered the site in the south-east corner of Trafalgar Square on the opposite side of Nelson's Column

Sir Henry Havelock's statue was sculpted by William Behnes (1795–1864) who made a speciality of portrait busts, particularly of children. Despite his great success he ended up destitute and died in Middlesex Hospital after, according to one source, having been found in the gutter.

to that of Napier's monument for a statue to Havelock whose death was deeply mourned. The money for it was raised by public subscription and the commission went to William Behnes who completed it in 1861.

In recent times there have been left-wing calls for Napier and Havelock to be at best relocated, at worst destroyed, on the grounds that they are either irrelevant or emblematic of a history in which there is nothing to celebrate. In 1999, however, Paul Usherwood of *Art Monthly* made the important point that, along with Nelson, 'in their day they were regarded as a new breed of national hero fit for the new kind of non-dynastic, meritocratic conception of Britain…the inscriptions tell of individual worth rather than property or ancestry'.

The man who discovered vaccination

The statue of the great physician, Edward Jenner (1749–1823) by William Calder Marshall (1818–1878), was intended to occupy a permanent place in the Square, and given the importance of his contribution to medical advancement and the proximity of the Royal College of Physicians, it must have seemed fitting. Queen Victoria had approved the proposal; Prince Albert had inaugurated the statue in 1858. But there were many who felt that Trafalgar Square should be kept as a place for military heroes, not doctors, and pressure in both the press and Parliament led to its relocation to Kensington Gardens four years later. By this time Prince Albert was dead, the Queen had given herself up to mourning: Jenner's admirers could not enlist royal support for his cause. *Punch* produced a satirical quatrain on the subject:

England's ingratitude still blots
The escutcheon of the brave and free;
I saved you many millions of spots.
And now you grudge one spot for me.

Outgrowing the space

The first changes were soon taking place to the surrounding buildings. In 1852 the Commissioners of HM Woods, Forests and Land Revenues had approved the construction of an extension to the Union Club in the form of an extra floor in the centre of the building.

The National Gallery was always hungry for additional space. Expecting the Gallery and the Royal Academy to share the same building had been unreasonable from the outset, and the latter institution had been looking for separate accommodation. Burlington House was in prospect, but in the interim some £15,000 of mainly temporary internal alterations were begun towards the end of 1860. The Gallery closed in the October, expecting to re-open a couple of months later. Unfortunately, the work also included some new roofing, and a severe winter delayed the contractors by six months.

In place of a central hall, long considered dark and useless, the Royal Academy gained a much enlarged sculpture room while above it the National Gallery at last acquired another generous exhibition space with smaller ante-rooms lit by glass panels rather than lanterns. Rather than entering by the steps to the portico, visitors to the Gallery went in through a side door on the west side. When the building re-opened in May 1861 the public was able to enjoy not only the original pictures but three recently acquired works by Fra Angelico, Rogier Van der Weyden and Piero della Francesca.

Lord Dover's ideal of bringing art within the reach of a far wider public was being realised, but by now there was a concurrent agenda. Just as Trafalgar Square was intended as a national icon and proof to foreign visitors of British supremacy, so the National Gallery was expected to play its part by competing successfully against its main European rivals. The vigorous policy of acquisition would continue, with some notable

additions and, inevitably, several missed opportunities. Some years later, when *The Times* celebrated the purchase of Antonello da Messina's *Portrait of an Unknown Man* in the kind of depth that today's newspapers reserve for the latest Hollywood blockbuster, the reviewer could not refrain from lamenting that the Renaissance master's finest portrait was in the Louvre. He then savagely castigated the Gallery and the government which funded it for failing to secure a recently auctioned Raphael, particularly because that painting had now joined 14 other Raphaels already at the Louvre. London, he pointed out, only had three, half as many as St Petersburg, and less even than the much newer Berlin gallery.

Nor had critical opinion grown any fonder of the edifice that housed the national collection than it had been when it was first constructed. Five years later, in 1866, a limited competition was held in which 10 architects, including Charles Barry junior and his brother Edward, were invited to submit designs for a completely new building. No commission was awarded but two years later still Edward Barry (1830–1880) was given the job of extending but not changing Wilkins' building.

In 1869 the National Gallery and Royal Academy finally parted company. The Royal Academy moved out to its present home, Burlington House, Piccadilly. By 1876 Barry had added another eight rooms, the first large-scale extension to Wilkins' original building. These being on the north side of the gallery, on the site of the old St Martin's workhouse, they did not affect the view from the Square, but they did give the gallery 20 exhibition rooms decorated in the rich, deep colours that were so popular in the late Victorian period.

Further extensions and remodelling followed rapidly, including the redesign of the staircase by Sir John Taylor (1833–1912), and shortly after the First World War the Gallery was unusual in that it hung its paintings in a single row.

No matter how quickly the National Gallery added extensions it could barely keep pace with the increase in its collection, whether from its own purchases or from generous gifts such as the Vernon, Wynn Ellis and Turner bequests. By the time Henry Tidmarsh painted this view of the steps in 1883, Edward Barry's 1876 extension was already insufficient.

CHAPTER 4 THE HEART OF THE CAPITAL

Northumberland Avenue

A major change was about to take place 'across the road' that would totally alter the view from the Gallery portico. Since 1605 the great Jacobean mansion of the Dukes of Northumberland had dominated the Strand at Charing Cross. In 1865 there was a proposal to build a road that would join Trafalgar Square to the new Victoria Embankment. At that time the Duke did not wish to sell the property, but three years later a disastrous fire swept through a significant part of the house, and in 1873 the purchase was concluded. Such deals were usually done by a species of compulsory purchase, so that the Metropolitan Board of Works bought up all the property in the area, completed their changes and then sold off or leased such land as they did not need. Ralph Turvey argues in *The Economics of Real Property* that in all but one case the Board came off financially worse. That one exception was the creation of Northumberland Avenue. In this case only 47 freeholds, leases or tenancies had to be purchased to gain a 4-acre site because the Duke's house occupied so much of the land and the Duke himself was anxious not to be seen to profit unfairly. He was paid £497,000, and by 1876 Northumberland Avenue had created two wedge-shaped sites pointing towards the Square.

The land between the Strand and Northumberland Avenue was taken for one of the new luxury hotels springing up in the West End, the Grand Hotel, with the Constitutional Club behind it. Externally it was unimpressive: 'a shapeless pile which from the Trafalgar Square side looks like a rounded bastion pierced with innumerable loop holes'. Inside, it was a different matter: a luxurious English hotel at last capable of competing with the best in the world and even with diffused electric lighting. The delightfully eccentric gourmet, traveller and writer, Lieutenant-Colonel Nathaniel Newnham-Davis of the East Kent Regiment described it in 1899 in *Dinners and Diners*.

OPPOSITE The Venetian artist Canaletto executed this view of Northumberland House in 1752 during a long and profitable business trip to England in which he painted numerous stately homes. Opposite the mansion stands the Golden Cross and other buildings which had all been demolished long before the axe fell on the oldest building on the Square.

RIGHT The Grand Hotel rose up on the site of Northumberland House between the Strand and the new Northumberland Avenue. A room at the luxury establishment cost from 3s 6d (17.5p) to 15/- (75p) per day; a three-bedroom suite with bathroom and drawing room between 3 and 4 guineas. Fires were extra. Guests received a visitor's booklet which included details of tariffs, church services, embassies, cab fares and sending or receiving telegrams. Suppliers such as the Anglo American Brush Electric Light Corp. Ltd invited guests to visit their factory.

hall, which has pillars of white and black marble, is handsome, and has absorbed what was once the reading-room. Should you desire to give a family dinner during your stay…there is a very delightful suite of rooms, known as the Walnut Rooms, where the head cook of the hotel – who previously cooked for the members of that politically misguided, but excellently appointed club, the Reform – has had the honour of serving meals to princes of the Royal blood. As for the company at the Grand, I should take it that it is chiefly of old country families, or the heads of great firms in the North.

And for those who could run to 5/- (25p) for a meal it was possible to dine at the table d'hôte, an idea imported from the continent, as well as à la carte, not only at the Grand but at the Victoria and the Metropole. The last two hotels occupied a large part of the second triangular site – between the western side of Northumberland Avenue and the pre-existing Whitehall, most of whose buildings survived intact.

The less wealthy tourists, who wanted their view of the Square without paying the Grand's prices, could continue to enjoy more modest accommodation at the very popular Morley's Hotel, 'an edifice about half windows where the plebeian traveller may sit and contemplate Northumberland House', as Oliver Wendell Holmes described it – at least until the demolition of that mansion obliged the same tourist to stare enviously at the Grand.

I inspected the sitting-rooms on the first floor, and saw some, notably a room decorated in white colour, with a fine view over the Square, and well within hearing of the bells of the neighbouring church, which would suit you admirably. But Miss Judith might prefer the stir and gaiety of the public rooms to a private apartment, and the great dining-room with its white marble pillars with gold capitals, its mirrors set in a frame of deep-coloured velvets, its roof of stained glass, its many tables covered with white napery, is a most chaste yet withal cheerful apartment. A smaller dining-room in which alabaster pillars support the roof is also a delightful room. The

Rights and riots

But this concentration of wealth and high art was in marked contrast to the poverty and ignorance that still existed in the vicinity. John Nash may have thought that he could exclude the poorest classes from the area, but he was wrong: the Square attracted the destitute as well as the affluent and at night they could be found sleeping rough. A period of relative economic affluence had come to an end by 1880 and those at the bottom of

the economic heap, many of them packed into the squalor of East End lodging houses and tenements, had descended from simple poverty into a wretchedness hard to imagine. Using data presented to the Royal Statistical Society in 1887 by Charles Booth, Gary Wroe calculated that around 117,000 East Enders were estimated to be not just poor but on the edge of starvation. Low wages in the docks and the sweatshops, insecure work and long-term unemployment were leading to unrest among those worst affected, and to action by those who had enough of a conscience to

articulate their grievances for them. Establishment fears of revolt led to certain marches or rallies in locations such as Trafalgar Square being banned, and, with street gatherings illegal, people had, in practice, nowhere to express their views. It made little difference that the vast majority of demonstrations or meetings had been notable by their peacefulness: fear of 'the mob' was real in what was a very anxious age.

A demonstration in February 1886 had resulted in civil unrest when three groups of protestors, the London United Workers

Committee, the Social Democratic League and a large number of the unemployed came to the Square to protest. The first group had secured permission for a peaceful demonstration but, unnerved by the numbers, the police had persuaded the Social Democratic League to march off to Hyde Park. On the way windows in the gentlemen's clubs were smashed and Oxford Street, already a thriving retail centre, saw damage to well-known stores as well as assaults on people in the vicinity. Frederick Engels, the businessman and philosophical communist who worked closely with Karl Marx, suspected that the police had deliberately allowed the trouble to get out of hand; a committee of inquiry blamed the police organisation, and the Chief Commissioner resigned on a golden handshake.

But the worst violence ever seen in Trafalgar Square was to take place at the end of the following year during a protest that would not be rivalled for just over a century. A demonstration in support of the unemployed in England and civil rights in Ireland was called for Trafalgar Square on Sunday, 13 November. It was prohibited: all demonstrations in the Square were banned following the 1886 incident, and on the day the Square was packed with police. Special Constables had been enrolled and the Life Guards were in reserve.

As the demonstrators, variously numbered but possibly about 20,000–30,000, neared the Square violence broke out. The armed police went after the protestors' banners, who in turn hit back with whatever sticks and piping they had been able to get their hands on. At about 4 p.m. six horse-drawn wagons – one of them carrying a band and the rest full of protestors – came towards the Square from the north. This coincided with an attempt by a group on foot to reach the Square from near Morley's Hotel. The police horses charged into the fray and two of the leaders of the protest were arrested including the MP Cunninghame Graham. Charing Cross hospital filled up with the wounded but there is no firm confirmation that anyone died.

A week later, it was a different story. Alfred Linnell, an impoverished law-writer was in Trafalgar Square at the same time as the police were clearing it of demonstrators sympathetic to a big Hyde Park demonstration against poverty that was taking place. Indignant at the police tactics, he and the group around him started to heckle, and he was ridden down by a mounted policeman close by the statue of Charles I. His thigh crushed, he was eventually taken to hospital, not by the authorities but by members of the public. Blood poisoning set in and his subsequent

death became a cause célèbre. All sorts of stories circulated about the cause of his death and even about the place where he died. It was alleged that he was drunk, which his employer refuted; and the inquest was adjourned in order, many suspected, that his corpse would decay and need a swift burial. His supporters, however, circumvented that eventuality by the use of a hermetically sealed coffin, and a massive funeral was planned. At the last moment, police permission to start from the statue of Charles I was withdrawn. Nevertheless, thousands lined the streets and followed the cortege. A pamphlet was issued by William Morris and others to be sold for the benefit of Linnell's orphans who had been placed in the workhouse by his brother-in-law after Linnell had been widowed. The pamphlet included a grim hymn penned by Morris with music by Malcolm Lawson.

The plight of the poor elicited little local sympathy. Ratepayers from St Martin's and St James's parishes organised a petition – which the gentlemen of the Union Club refused to sign – complaining that the 'spasmodic and almost daily progress of disorderly mobs mainly composed of those known to the law as thieves and vagabonds through the streets on which their business premises front' was seriously affecting their trade. And while the demonstrators had complained of police brutality, the ratepayers thought the police were being restrained by their superiors. Individuals also wrote: the manager of the Grand Hotel, Robert Holland, stated that customers were leaving early, cancelling advance reservations and telling him that their friends were simply not coming at all. The Treasurer of the Royal College of Physicians wrote darkly to Police Commissioner Sir Charles Warren that 'to have the lions and steps of Nelson's monument made a playground for idle young lads from day to day is simply disgraceful and argues fatuous feebleness in some quarter'.

Homelessness became a popular theme for the Music Hall, the cheery couplets masking the grim reality of a winter's night in a city square.

I live in Trafalgar Square
with four lions to guard me.
Fountains and statues all over the place,
And the metropolis staring me right in the face.
I'll own it's a trifle draughty,
But I look at it this way, you see:
If it's good enough for Nelson,
It's quite good enough for me.
The beds ain't so soft as they might be,
Still, the temperature's never too high.
And it's nice to see the swells who are passing
Look on you with envious eyes.
(From 'I live in Trafalgar Square')

Gordon of Khartoum

Along with the homeless, another temporary resident came to the Square when a statue to Sir Charles Gordon, 'Gordon of Khartoum', was erected between the fountains in 1888. Like Henry Havelock, Gordon (1833–1885) became a committed Christian; a man who refused rewards, reduced his pay, spent his own money on his troops, suppressed the slave trade in Equatoria and Dafur and believed that he was doing God's work. Unlike Havelock, he was a tortured soul, struggling to repress sexual feelings, and his philanthropic work among the poor of Gravesend included a tender interest – there is no proof that a stronger word should be used – in the orphan boys for whom he cared.

His reputation as a soldier was made in China during the early 1860s when he took charge of the 4000 Imperial Chinese soldiers trying to protect the international settlement at Shanghai against Taiping insurgents.

In 1881 public opinion demanded that Gordon, by now a national hero in the same league as Nelson, be sent to the Sudan he knew so well, this time to deal with a revolt led by the Mahdi. He went, and for more than 300 days he held Khartoum. By the

time the government sent a relieving force, the city had fallen and Gordon had been killed.

At home he was hailed as a martyr, his death, a stain on the nation. Small wonder that his statue, by Sir W Hamo Thorneycroft (1850–1925), found its place between the fountains of Trafalgar Square. In 1943 it had to be moved, but after the war it failed to reappear and now stands on the Victoria Embankment.

Admiralty Arch

Victoria's reign had been the longest and, in terms of the changes, good and bad, over which she presided, among the most dramatic in British history. It was to be commemorated in the form of a massive sculpture outside Buckingham Palace and the construction of a processional route through St James's Park to Trafalgar Square – The Mall. The road scheme had been proposed much earlier; Victoria's death in 1901 gave it an impetus. Buildings near the Square were to be demolished, and in their place a triumphal archway designed by Sir Aston Webb (1849–1930) would form a majestic gateway to the park – Admiralty Arch. The former pupil of Charles Barry junior, Webb was the leading architect of his day, confident in an eclectic range of styles and skilful in big commissions.

Webb faced two problems with the project. One was the axis. Without wholesale demolitions in the Trafalgar Square area,

The best view of Admiralty Arch, as in this 1909 pencil and watercolour by Robert Atkinson, is from above, where the convex curves of the flanking buildings flow into its concave wings. Drummond's Bank frames the left-hand side; that on the right has been replaced by the Malaysian Tourist Board and Uganda High Commission.

Nobody knows exactly what became of this drinking fountain after it was removed from Battersea Park. Suspicions are that it lies at the bottom of the Thames. It commemorated the anonymous mongrel which galvanised the anti-vivisection movement and prompted a riot in Trafalgar Square. (Courtesy of Patrick Loobey)

including Drummond's Bank, a straight road from the Palace, through the Arch and into the Strand was impossible. Since such demolition was unfeasible, Webb's monument would have to disguise the abrupt change of axis, and this he solved practically, by securing agreement to demolish three offices on the opposite side of the road to Drummond's, and artistically, with the two great concave wings to the massive arch. Unusually for a memorial, Admiralty Arch was not simply a monument: it provided the London residences for two Sea Lords and office accommodation for Admiralty staff.

The second difficulty he encountered was with London County Council, who took exception to footing the bill for changes to the road on the Charing Cross side of the Arch – not just the road widening but the cost of compensating the companies who would lose their offices. Between 1896 and 1909 property prices had risen sharply; the Council pointed out that if the Office of Works had involved them at an early stage they could have made the purchases well in advance of the rises. Relations between the two bodies grew increasingly acrimonious during 1910, with Webb left powerless. Another great scheme was turning into farce, and the death of Edward VII created a new imperative: to have the scheme completed in time for the coronation of George V the following year. As the impasse, now involving Westminster Council, continued, an exasperated George Drummond went to see Webb and offered to donate some of the Bank's land to the Council if it would set back the three buildings opposite, an offer the Council subsequently rejected. It was not until May 1912 that the three buildings, including the old Phoenix Assurance, were demolished, and even as the masonry came down a large compensation claim by Commercial Union was under binding arbitration.

London Underground

One of the most fundamental changes to London had taken place largely out of sight: the building of the London Underground. First to be constructed was the Metropolitan Line, followed by the District Line, and in 1906 the Bakerloo line opened – officially, the Baker Street-to-Waterloo Line. This enabled travellers to alight at Trafalgar Square station on the south-eastern side of the Square by Morley's Hotel and the Charing Cross Post Office which occupied part of the southern end of the hotel building. The station still exists, but during the 1970s the public had to navigate a string of name changes among the London Underground stations in the vicinity of Charing Cross. In 1976, Charing Cross Underground reverted to its 1906 name of Embankment and three years later Trafalgar Square became Charing Cross, although the platform roundels still reassuringly include the words 'for Trafalgar Square'.

Vivisection and votes for women

In the early years of the twentieth century, Socialism was not the only cause out on the Square. Vivisection, as controversial then as now, was a subject that had been brought to the attention of the public and Parliament during the last quarter of the previous century, but in 1907 violence erupted over a statue erected in Battersea to a small mongrel. The statue had been funded by the International Anti-Vivisection Society, two of whose members had infiltrated a lecture at which they had been appalled by the experiments performed on what was to become known as 'The Brown Dog'. The statue carried an inflammatory inscription stating that the dog had been 'done to death in the laboratories of University College in February, 1903, after having endured vivisection extending over more than two months and having been handed over from one vivisector to another till death came to his release'.

The statue required 24-hour guard, and by November 1807 the courts were having to deal with charges of assault, obstructing the police, criminal damage and breaches of the peace: the accused being students from either side of the argument. On 12 December up to 400 medical students went to Trafalgar Square shouting, 'Brown Dog, hurrah!', and also protesting against the recent conviction of some of their comrades. This in itself was a breach of the law, which allowed authorised protests only on Saturday afternoons and Sundays. The police dispersed the crowd but it reassembled and, by the time the police had gained control at 2 a.m., 12 people had been arrested.

The matter only ended when, in 1911, a newly elected Council ordered the destruction of the monument, but visitors to Battersea Park today will find a modern statue to the Brown Dog erected 20 years ago by Ken Livingstone's Greater London Council.

Perhaps the most high-profile campaign of the Edwardian era was that aimed at giving women the vote. Suffragists had been demanding this for many years, but the formation in 1903 of the Women's Social and Political Union (WSPU) – nicknamed the Suffragettes in 1906 by the *Daily Mail* – raised the stakes.

Frustrated by the defeat of every peaceful move to enfranchise women, the WSPU advocated direct action: civil disobedience and criminal damage. Led by Annie Kenny and Emmeline Pankhurst they burned down churches, chained themselves to railings, invaded the Houses of Parliament, attacked Churchill, deliberately assaulted policemen and generally ensured that their cause remained in the public eye.

Trafalgar Square was inevitably a focal point for their rallies, although the biggest had to be held at Hyde Park; one 1908 rally may have attracted over 400,000. These meetings tended to be peaceful: the women came to listen to their leaders and trouble was more likely to be caused by their opponents who turned up to heckle. Nor were they all WSPU gatherings. The Women's

Suffragette Christabel Pankhurst addresses supporters from the base of Nelson's Column on Sunday, 11 October 1908 urging them to come unarmed and help rush the House of Commons on the Tuesday. Along with her mother, Emmeline, and Mrs Drummond, she was brought to trial on charges including, 'inciting the public to do a certain wrongful and illegal act'.

To maintain or increase morale during the First World War, captured weapons, in this case artillery, were shipped back to England and put on display to suggest that the troops were making advances.

Freedom League met around Nelson's Column in 1909 to bury the mock-up of a coffin symbolically beneath a white shroud bearing the words 'Killed by the Government', a reference to the shelved Women's Emancipation Bill of that year. Protestors came to London from across the country: a 1906 rally was convened by women from Cheshire, Lancashire, Salford and Manchester – largely textile workers – and addressed by, among others, the sympathetic MP T F Richards. There were also many women who had no desire for the vote, and they took their anti-suffrage campaign to Trafalgar Square.

Suffragette militancy brought about the temporary closure of the National Gallery and the Wallace Collection in 1914 after damage to exhibits at the Royal Academy, the British Museum and the National Gallery. The National Gallery suffered the most, through a frenzied axe attack on Velasquez's *Rokeby Venus* by the Canadian-born Mary Richardson.

Upon the outbreak of the First World War most campaigners abandoned militancy and put their energies behind the war effort. Women eventually gained the vote after the war. Historians still debate how far the violence of the WSPU delayed or accelerated the granting of the franchise.

Bensley's bet

Trafalgar Square had its lighter moments. Anyone crossing the Square at 10.30 a.m. on New Year's Day 1908 and seeing a man wearing a metal mask and pushing a pram bearing the text 'walking round the world – a £21,000 wager', might have been forgiven for wondering whether they had celebrated a little too

During the war years Trafalgar Square was conscripted into service. Fundraising and morale-boosting events were regularly held to bring people closer to the war without, of course, giving any hint of the obscenely high death tolls and the appalling conditions on the Western Front. Civilians and potential recruits were asked to admire the hardware that turned warfare into mechanised slaughter.

much the night before. But Harry Bensley, a wealthy Thetford playboy with investments in Russia, was out to win the largest single bet ever recorded. Lord Lonsdale (of Lonsdale Belt fame) and J Pierpont Morgan, the American millionaire, had argued at their club over whether a man could walk round the world without being identified, and Bensley had interrupted them to say it was and he would prove it. The bet with Morgan was on, but with a few conditions attached: Bensley had to wear a helmet from a suit of armour and push a pram. He could start out with only £1, and any expenses had to be financed from the sale of a stock of postcards of him wearing his helmet. On the journey he had to find

a wife (rather tricky since research suggests he was already married), and he could only take a change of underwear. For six years Bensley and a paid companion followed the agreed route across 30,000 miles, taking in New York and Sydney, until with just 7000 miles to go they reached Genoa. There they learned that war had been declared. The bet was off and Bensley returned home, but Morgan gave him £4000, which he in turn donated to charity.

First World War

Seen in retrospect, there was a dreadful inevitability about the First World War: the culmination of an arms race and of a stack of

Immortalised in plays, novels and folksongs, the recruiting sergeant was a familiar figure in towns and villages, particularly in time of war. Two centuries after the Battle of Blenheim, when the Rochester recruiting sergeant marched through the town beating his kettledrum and calling on young men to 'come be a soldier', he still had an important role.

international alliances that allowed the Sarajevo assassination to lock Europe into a conflict unlike any other in history. Even so, the speed of events took many by surprise. Only four days before the Germans marched into Belgium in order to avoid French defences on the Franco-German border, a TUC sponsored rally in Trafalgar Square was urging the government not to get involved in a war but to do all it could to achieve peace. But once Belgian neutrality had been violated war was declared. Almost the entire country threw itself patriotically into the struggle believing that if they had not yet liberated Belgium they had captured the moral high ground. Hundreds of thousands queued to enlist or pledged their willingness to join up when required.

Many soldiers passed through Trafalgar Square on their way to and from Charing Cross rail station and found an unexpected place in which to shelter for the night. St Martin-in-the-Fields followed the lead of its patron saint, Martin of Tours. When approached one winter's day by a beggar in threadbare rags, Martin, with no money to give the man, tore his cloak in half and shared it. That night, he had a vision and understood that the beggar was Christ. And so the Reverend Dick Sheppard, one of the most influential churchmen of his day, threw open the church's crypt to the cold and weary soldiers, the beginning of a social care programme that would develop in size and professionalism over the decades to come.

Facing up to the threat of aerial attack for the first time, the National Gallery was one of several institutions that evacuated works of art. Choosing to make its own arrangements, it negotiated with the London Electric Company and sent about 300 paintings to the safety of Aldwych Underground station. After Zeppelin attacks in the Essex/East London area, the Office of Works encased the statue of Charles I in sandbags and corrugated iron, but the Square was spared the bomb attacks that would come 25 years later.

Even so, the Square had a part to play. Captured enemy weaponry was exhibited to keep up morale, and in 1917 open-air entertainment was provided for wounded soldiers and those on leave in London. This was the brainchild of Andrew Fisher, the High Commissioner for Australia, and took the form of music by the Coldstream Guards and what was described as a 'cinematograph exhibition'. Films were projected from a lantern on a lorry on the terrace down on to a stage in the Square that had been draped with a black cloth. Footage of Anzac troops and food production was interspersed with statements from, among others, the Prime Minister, who exhorted people to unite in the cause. Speakers made short speeches, and the whole programme was repeated at two-hourly intervals.

Before the introduction of conscription, recruiting rallies were held, vividly described by Lieutenant John Patrick Teahan, a young Canadian commissioned into the Sherwood Foresters who had no illusions about the war, calling it: 'not war at all, but a series of long-distance murders'. On leave in London during August 1916 he observed:

Recruiting goes merrily on. In Trafalgar Square immense crowds gather at the Nelson column while sergeants and officers harangue them from the steps and soldiers pass through the crowd urging men to Come up to the Colours, like a Salvation Army revival where people are pleaded with to

come up and be saved. Every once in a while, some civilian who can no longer stand the pressure mounts the steps and accepts the King's shilling while the band plays and exhorters testify: 'Join now, boys, and spend a delightful winter in the trenches!'

Two months later Teahan was missing in action, presumed dead.

The horrific death toll in the trenches forced the army to recruit women for the first time, to replace men doing so-called 'soft' jobs who could then be sent to fight. The Women's Auxiliary Army Corps (WAAC) was founded in January 1917 and thousands of women joined up to take on what were considered suitable tasks for their gender, such as administrative and catering positions. But they were not beyond the reach of the German guns and did sustain losses, which their brilliant Administrator, Helen Gwynne-Vaughan, regarded as perfectly legitimate in war. After the war the WAAC was renamed Queen Mary's Army Auxiliary Corps, with the Queen herself as Commandant-in-Chief. By this stage, Gwynne-Vaughan, soon to be appointed Professor of Botany at Birkbeck College and later created a Dame, had been reassigned to take charge of the Women's Royal Air Corps (WRAC).

Money as well as personnel was needed. Campaigns, which included large-scale publicity stunts, regularly encouraged the population to purchase War Bonds. Trafalgar Square underwent a spectacular transformation at the beginning of October 1918 into a war-shattered French village. Twenty thousand sandbags created the trenches; a ruined church tower covered the statue of Gordon; one fountain became a broken down windmill, the other was hidden beneath a heavily shelled French farmhouse. The wall at the north end supported the painting of a war-torn landscape, and artillery lined up facing the National Gallery. The public could walk through the sanitised trench environment much as if they were in a modern, hands-on museum and have their Bonds specially stamped in one of the field guns adapted for the purpose.

The Women's Auxiliary Army Corps also went out recruiting in Trafalgar Square, but their sergeants were called forewomen – not even the two most senior officers were allowed to hold commissions; they were called administrators. The WAAC was an unqualified success and another step on the road to women's equality.

CHAPTER 5 CELEBRATION AND PROTEST

OPPOSITE By the end of the twentieth century major changes had taken place in and around the Square. Major new buildings were erected, and diplomacy replaced the Union Club, the Royal College of Physicians and Morley's Hotel. The National Gallery continued its expansion, St Martin's became famous not just for its architecture and early radio broadcasts but for its social care programme, and for a few cold weeks each year the Norwegian Christmas tree relegated Nelson to second place. Additional memorials arrived; fierce arguments erupted over the still-vacant fourth plinth; new gen-erations of protestors with new causes to fight for took over the space for high-profile demonstrations. Election nights, coronations and royal weddings packed thousands into the Square. The advent of the 'big screen' allowed more people than ever before to participate in national events.

RIGHT George Washington's statue, which stands on the grass terrace immediately in front of the National Gallery, has sometimes raised eyebrows among those who believe the Square should be for the British. Although he fought against the British and led the American colonies to independence, Washington was English by birth, which sets an interesting precedent.

On the night of 10 November 1920 groups of people stood in mute respect on wet railway platforms between Victoria Station and Dover. Residents whose houses overlooked the line gazed out of upstairs windows to watch a train race past. The next morning – Armistice Day – one of the largest crowds ever to assemble in Trafalgar Square waited in silence as the cortege bearing the body of the Unknown Warrior passed by on its way to the Cenotaph and then to burial in Westminster Abbey. Many of those who lined the route had been there all night, and after the ceremony some 40,000 people visited the Abbey, while even after midnight thousands more queued from Trafalgar Square down Whitehall to contemplate at the Cenotaph. Over a million people paid their respects during the three days of official pilgrimage, and many came afterwards. The spontaneous outpouring of emotion was unprecedented and probably remains unequalled.

The idea of commemorating one anonymous soldier in honour of the thousands who had no known grave had come from the Reverend David Railton MC who, as a padre in France in 1916, had been profoundly moved by a grave at his billet in Armentières marked with a simple cross. In black pencil was written, 'An Unknown British Soldier', and underneath in brackets, 'Of the Black Watch'.

Foreign friends around the Square

If fascism became the enemy in the 1930s, Russian Bolshevism was the bogeyman of the 1920s, at least among the Establishment, and a speech in front of the National Gallery in 1921 underlined the notion of an Anglo-American front against the threat. The speaker was Henry Louis Smith, President of Washington and Lee University, and he had come to unveil a bronze copy of Jean-Antoine Houdon's (1741–1828) marble statue of George Washington at Richmond, Virginia.

…we hereby present to the government and people of Great Britain this bronze likeness of one who forsook her flag, rejected her sovereignty and fought against her king.

ABOVE A wave of inflation was said to have hit commercial property prices in central London when it was known that the Canada High Commission was in the market for a prestigious location. They settled on – and into – the Union Club, turning the smoking room into the High Commissioner's office.

LEFT For the 1937 coronation of King George VI the Canadians erected this massive covered grandstand against their building to accommodate their guests. Staff can also be seen up on the roof and even on the portico as a body of the Royal Canadian Mounted Police pass the High Commission.

And…she answers the challenge by placing this one-time rebel on a pedestal amid the mighty monuments and memories of Trafalgar Square.

Smith ended his speech with a rousing call to Britain to stand with America against Bolshevism, which his country then regarded as the greatest evil threatening the world.

Before too long George Washington was not the only permanent North American fixture on the Square. The Union Club, with only a limited lease left on Smirke's building, was open to offers, and the one it found it could not refuse came from the Government of Canada. Ottawa paid £225,000 for the building and £2000 a year for a 40-year lease. In the words of the delighted Canadian Premier, Mackenzie King, The High Commissioner, The Honourable Peter Larkin, who had spent months scouting for a building, had 'really scored in a big way'.

Major refurbishment was undertaken before the Canadians moved in. The trappings of the Club, its billiard room, antiquated heating and inadequate telephones system were taken out; native Canadian woods were imported; and internal walls were moved to create offices and reception rooms of the appropriate size. Significant changes to the exterior of the building also took place. The entrance was changed to the Cockspur Street: out went the bow window and in came a portico similar to that at the Royal College of Physicians. The original entrance on to the Square was blocked up and refaced to match the other half of the building and another floor was added, a move that destroyed the proportions of the edifice. Although known as Canada House, the façade sports only the name 'Canada' in gold letters – both Premier King and High Commissioner Larkin felt that 'House' was demeaning.

With its prestigious location the Canadian diplomats no longer had to look enviously at other embassies as they had done from their cramped offices in Victoria Street. When King George V and Queen Mary came to open the building in June 1925, the King is said to have told Larkin, in private, that his office was finer than that of any other High Commissioner – finer than his own, in fact. Yet even as the new occupants settled in they were casting acquisitive eyes on the rest of Smirke's building.

The Canadians were not the first, however, to set up their High Commission on the Square. South Africa had also been looking for a new home. In 1921 they had taken a lease on Morley's Hotel on the opposite side. There was already a tenuous African connection with the area where, a little over 150 years earlier, in the days of the Golden Cross, a rhinoceros had been exhibited. Shortly after the High Commission was installed, Pretoria bought the building and gained permission to demolish it. This was to be the first, and last, wholesale reconstruction on the Square itself.

Sir Herbert Baker (1862–1946), who had worked successfully in both South Africa and India, was expected to design a building that would not only be functional, symbolic and aesthetically pleasing, but which would sit comfortably alongside the existing architecture, both in terms of style and scale. Setting aside personal preferences, he deferred to St Martin's and the National Gallery, proposing a Corinthian colonnade on the Trafalgar Square elevation that made a connection with the two dominant buildings, a connection emphasised by the prescribed use of Portland stone. The narrow southern elevation would echo that of Canada House.

Baker's original mansard roof was vetoed by the Royal Fine Arts Commission (RFAC) but, with support from the British Prime Minister and the High Commissioner, he successfully held out for his colonnade to which the RFAC objected on the grounds that it was so much higher than that of Canada House. At the time, Baker was under the impression that the Canadians planned to rebuild, which they did not.

Surprisingly – given past experience – the demolition of Morley's Hotel and the construction of South Africa House took

After two years as the South Africa High Commission, Morley's Hotel was pulled down. Like the Grand on the other side of the Strand it had outlived its time as a hotel.

This view of South Africa House shows the Corinthian colonnade on the Trafalgar Square side of the building and the narrow southern elevation. Baker had actually developed the whole site between Duncannon Street and the Strand, the remainder of the building carries the evocative name of Golden Cross House.

View down the Strand into Trafalgar Square in the early 1920s. On the left side stands the famous Lyon's Corner House which provided cheap food for visitors and whose name revives memories of childhood visits to London as late as the 1960s. On the opposite side is Morley's Hotel, extending over the ground-floor shops – which would soon be demolished to make way for South Africa House.

just over two years, during which time a hoarding once again allowed bill posters free rein to advertise the great variety of entertainment on offer in the metropolis. By July 1932 the building was perfectly recognisable.

If Baker's basic design owed everything to Trafalgar Square, the external sculpture and the whole of the interior was pure colonial South Africa, for Baker believed in sentiment and symbols. The indefatigable Yorkshire architect, Joseph Armitage (1880–1945), was responsible not just for the Corinthian capitals but also for almost all the African flora and fauna that decorate the exterior.

The most obvious piece of sculpture, the gilded bronze Winged Springbok, was executed by Sir Charles Wheeler (1892–1974), although the idea came from Baker. The latter had been inspired by the sight of a winged ibex among the Persian collection at the Louvre. He married this to the springbok, already an icon in South African sport, and so 'invented' a national symbol.

Carved on the pediment of the portico is the ship *Goede Hoop (Good Hope)*, one of the five vessels which brought the first permanent white settlers to the Cape under the leadership of Jan van Riebeek. A young and, at the time, completely unknown South African, Coert Steynberg (1905–1985), who had asked for the chance to do some work on the new building, saw off some very well-established compatriots to gain what was considered the single most prestigious commission: the statue of Bartholomew Diaz, which is situated in its own niche at the south-west side of the building.

Inside, frescoes, paintings, sculpture, tapestries, plaster, wrought iron and inlay by a large number of artists, several of them students, combine with native marbles and woods to express the history, geography and culture of the South Africa as the white rulers saw it. Overall, the building was criticised by those who saw it as unoriginal, too heavily influenced by its surroundings; but it was very quickly given Listed Building status.

Trafalgar Square.
Police Telephone in Lamp Pedestal

The smallest police box

The original main entrance to South Africa House was from Trafalgar Square; today it is from the Strand, closer to the Underground entrance and closer, also, to probably the smallest police box ever built, a monument to the proverb that necessity is the mother of invention.

After the war the police had erected a temporary police box by the Underground station from where an officer could call for assistance. In 1926 the imminent remodelling of the station entrance required the box to be relocated, but there were serious artistic concerns about putting such an object in the Square itself. Towards the end of November, Sir Lionel Edwards at the Office of Works wrote to Scotland Yard:

This sketch from the files of the Office of Works was probably the first visualisation of what the converted lamp-plinth might look like as a police box. In reality the entrance faces north-west rather than south-west as shown here.

As regards the telephone box in Trafalgar square, a brainwave has come to us: we think it might be possible to get the telephone box inside the great granite base of the big lamp at the end of the balustrade at either side of the Square. It would, of course, mean taking down the whole structure, carving out the core and providing a room inside…of sufficient size for your man to operate, together with observation holes.

This ingenious proposal met with approval from the RFAC and the drum from the lamp was duly taken away to be transformed. The police asked for electricity to be laid as well as phone lines, so they could install a light that would flash red whenever an officer used the phone. This was refused on the grounds of both taste and logistics, but a resolution was reached when responsibility for that one lamp was passed to the police. Powered by electricity, it could now flash as required – but without any change of colour. Rendered obsolete by short-wave radio and mobile phone technology, it can, nevertheless, be seen at the south-eastern corner in its new role as a broom cupboard for the Square's cleaners.

The inter-war years

After 40 years of service to its wealthy clients, the Grand Hotel closed its doors at the end of the summer of 1927. What had once been considered the height of luxury had become outmoded and inefficient. Guests now expected ensuite bathrooms with running water; owners were looking for the economies of scale and higher profits made possible by larger and more modern hotels. The great building with its carved female figures and classical ornamentation was sold, divided into offices, after which it became known as Grand Buildings, and allowed to decline.

Another and more obvious advance was the arrival in spring 1933 of the first traffic lights in the Square, courtesy of Liverpool's

Automatic Electric Co. Ltd (AEC). In a published report the company declared that the traffic gyrating clockwise round the Square:

…presents a problem in control that is probably not exceeded in any part of the world. Were the traffic composed entirely of private cars the problem would be easier but when it is appreciated that probably 50–60% of the vehicles are omnibuses or vehicles of a heavy type, the magnitude of the problem can perhaps be realised.

The volume of traffic was certainly high: more than 2000 vehicles per hour passed the National Gallery; almost 3000 passed Canada House. In setting up the lights, AEC studied the manual controls exercised by the traffic police on the grounds that after so many years they were likely to have worked out the optimum system.

Motorists, of course, deeply resented the signals; pedestrians apparently could not see them. Six months after the installation one local councillor called the Square 'almost a death trap' during a meeting of Westminster City Council. Replying to the debate, Councillor Edgson summarised the problem even as he expressed optimism for the future: 'When the public got more used to the scheme, and drivers became more considerate when the light changed from amber to green as the pedestrian was completing the crossing, matters would be easier'.

During the inter-war years some of the former soldiers who had passed through Trafalgar Square on their way to the Front now returned as homeless and unemployed. Their ranks were swelled by a number of women also sleeping rough. Once again St Martin's opened up its vaults to provide shelter. The refuge was run by just two policewomen from nearby Bow Street, and they kept order with whistles. There was at that time a general fear of white slavers kidnapping women to sell them into prostitution, and on one occasion a group of men did invade the vault, only to

Cheerful police officers make checks on the route past Trafalgar Square planned for King George V's Silver Jubilee Procession. On 6 May 1935, thousands of well-wishers shoehorned themselves into the Square; hundreds watched from rooftops; St John's Ambulance dealt with scores who fainted in the heat.

flee when the redoubtable guardians employed their whistles. As the economy picked up in the 1930s the numbers of rough sleepers decreased until by 1939 they were down to 40 or less.

Jellicoe and Beatty

Given the carnage of the trenches it is hardly surprising that no monument to any First World War general appeared in Trafalgar Square. Instead, the government found its heroes in the navy, in the shapes of Admirals Beatty and Jellicoe, two men who will forever be locked together in the public mind as participants in the Battle of Jutland on 31 May 1916. The last great engagement

between two battleship fleets was one that did not in the end change the strategic balance of power between Britain and Germany, and therefore left Britannia still ruling the waves, but the damage done by the Germans gave them some claim to victory. The subsequent war of words between rival supporters of the two British admirals has continued to this day.

David Beatty (1871–1936) was an atypical British admiral. The youngest since Nelson, he enjoyed a personal fortune and a dashing air, an image cultivated and strengthened by the liberties taken with regulation uniform. His coat had six rather than eight buttons and his cap with extra wide brim was, at least in

photographs, worn at a rakish angle. Every inch the commander of the equally dashing Battle Cruiser Group in 1914, he perhaps had more of Lord Cardigan than Lord Nelson about him but he and his ships did fire the imagination of the British public in the early years of the Great War.

At Jutland, Beatty was first into action, sweeping into the fray with his fast battle cruisers and after watching two of his great ships explode from shellfire within half an hour famously said: 'there seems to be something wrong with our bloody ships today'. He was to see another explode and sink and much more damage inflicted to his fleet before he achieved his objective of luring the German High Seas Fleet into range of Jellicoe's Grand Fleet.

John Rushworth Jellicoe (1859–1935), Beatty's chief, had been an administrator in the Admiralty prior to the war where he advocated 'big gun' ships used in great concentration. He was an obvious choice to take command of the Grand Fleet in 1914; the first time since the Spanish Armada in 1588 that one man was in command of the entire British Fleet. A great tactician, he spent many hours developing complex fleet tactics to deal with any situation. Due to being on station at Scapa Flow in the Orkneys, he was a much less public figure than Beatty, but it was accepted at the time that gunners were better trained in the main fleet than in Beatty's squadrons.

In the event, Jutland was disappointing because, having apparently fallen into Jellicoe's trap, the German fleet executed an exceptionally skilful manoeuvre to reverse its course and Jellicoe, fearful of torpedo attack, was forever criticised for not following up his advantage and pursuing them.

To be fair to Jellicoe, he was cautious because he had an awesome responsibility. Churchill said of him that 'he was the only man on either side who could have lost the war in an afternoon'.

Jellicoe became First Sea Lord after Jutland until retirement in 1917. He was succeeded as Commander-in-Chief of the Grand Fleet by Beatty, who in turn served as First Sea Lord for an unprecedented period between 1919 and 1927. The decisions to honour both men in Trafalgar Square were taken in 1935–6; what followed was reminiscent of the Nelson monument saga.

The idea of commissioning full statues à la Napier and Havelock was swiftly discounted (as was replacing the soldiers with the sailors). As F J Raby at the Office of Works put it: 'we are all tired of statues of men in uniform'. Instead, and despite the misgivings of the RFAC, which declared itself to be 'oppressed by the difficulty of the marriage of individual memorials with fountains', it was decided to commission Edwin Lutyens (1869–1944) to remodel the two fountains, dedicating one to each man. The original proposal – a larger than life-size portrait bust of each man in the centre of 'his' fountain – was later abandoned in favour of portrait busts standing on plinths against the north wall.

Lady Jellicoe was against the scheme from the start. 'I think', wrote Raby, 'that actually, what mainly was in her mind was a firm dislike of any memorial to her husband being set up so close to that of Lord Beatty'. Sir Charles Wheeler received his second Trafalgar Square commission when he was entrusted not just with the bust of Beatty but also with the bronze mermen, which form part of the statuary in Lutyens' fountains. William MacMillan (1887–1977) sculpted Jellicoe and the mermaids. The initial budget for the scheme was just under £18,000, but when the sculptors asked for a further £500 they found an unusually indulgent ear at the Office of Works. Raby told his superior: 'Our experience of sculptors is that, in their pardonable anxiety not to place any obstacles in the way of obtaining the commission, they do not always stop to think whether the figure they are proposing is really anything like what…they ought to ask'.

Trafalgar Square was closed as Barry's unspectacular fountains were taken down, and once again a hoarding took pride of place. It had been agreed that the fountains would not be erected anywhere else; the implication seems to be that they were to be destroyed, and yet ultimately they were donated to Canada by the National Art Collection Fund, one finding a home outside the Legislative Building in Regina.

The dismantling of the fountains caused considerable inconvenience to the Square's most numerous residents, many of which were obliged to fly over to St James's Park every time they wanted a drink.

As the Second World War was declared, work on the memorials was halted. With palpable sadness the Office of Works made careful notes on exactly what had been done to date and where everything was being stored, tidying up the file ready for whoever would pick up the project after the war – the duration and outcome of which they had no way of knowing.

Second World War preparations

The Second World War was to affect the Square far more than did the First, and if it is possible for a space to rise to the occasion, Trafalgar Square certainly did. Whether it was the sight of Nelson defiant against the sky, or the memory of how much that was central to the nation had taken place within its boundaries, Trafalgar Square achieved a truly iconic national status after 1939. Quite how iconic only emerged well after the war with the discovery that if his invasion plan had worked, Hitler would have taken Nelson and his column back to Berlin. Like Napoleon who temporarily robbed Venice of the bronze horses of St Mark, which the Venetians themselves had looted from Constantinople much earlier, Hitler understood the value of symbols.

Before the end of 1939 an air-raid shelter for 800 people was constructed on the Square towards the north wall; the Underground station had already been designated as capable of holding 1600. To avoid chaos at the busy station when only one entrance was open, London Transport, successor to the London Electric Company, instituted a 'keep left' system and grew increasingly irritated by the public's wilful refusal to comply with the notices. Two years into the war, London Transport was

experimenting with glow-in-the-dark paint to help people negotiate the entrance and stairs in the blackout. The crypt of St Martin's also became an air-raid shelter and a canteen for the troops passing through.

From across the road, in Grand Buildings, The Navy League appealed for donations of knitted items and board games to send to the ships, and in February 1940 men from HMS *Ajax* and HMS *Exeter* marched through London to celebrate the naval victory at the Battle of the River Plate, which ended in the scuttling of the German pocket-battleship *Graf Spee*. After gallantry medals were presented at Horse Guards Parade, the procession continued to Trafalgar Square, which had once again become the stage for parades, rallies and fund-raising events.

Those early months became known as the Phoney War because so little military action took place, and they passed without incident in London. Precautions were taken, nonetheless. At South Africa House, hundreds of sandbags were taken on to the roof. Only when the whole roof was covered did someone point out that, when it rained, the weight of the wet sandbags would be too much, so down they had to come. Windows were taped up and the basement became a shelter. Staff were also trained as air-raid personnel. During the war the High Commissions of Canada and South Africa became second homes for those of their nationals who found themselves in Britain, and both countries committed thousands of troops to the Allied cause.

Saving the paintings

The outbreak of war did not catch the National Gallery unawares. This time, contingency planning was under the centralised control of the Office of Works, which had drawn up plans to evacuate all works of art from the capital's museums and galleries; a register of suitable locations had been drawn up and a number of country house owners and institutions, several in Wales, had agreed to accommodate the evacuees.

Like Beatty, Sir John, later Earl Jellicoe, had joined the navy at 13. Shot in the lung in 1900, he carried the bullet for the rest of his life. He, too, was honoured by the Canadians by having a peak named after him in 1918. At 3098 metres, Mount Jellicoe, Alberta, is a little taller than Mount Beatty, which, given the sensibilities surrounding the subsequent creation of the Trafalgar Square memorials to the two admirals, was fortuitious.

The National Gallery closed on 23 August 1939 and the task of evacuation began. Loading bays and lifts now made it much easier to move paintings between floors and out of the building. Once packed into their special crates almost all the paintings would be transported by rail; the one that was to give the greatest headache was the massive Van Dyke portrait of Charles I on horseback, for which special arrangements, including the lowering of the road under a bridge, had to be made. By the evening of 2 September, only a day before war was formally declared, the National Gallery was all but empty. The consignment of 218 paintings, which arrived at Bangor on 3 September was the most valuable cargo ever transported on a British train.

In June 1940, France fell to the Germans. With French airfields now at their disposal, the Luftwaffe were within easy range of London, which became a key target. That had serious implications for the National Gallery whose decision to move the country's art treasures to private houses had not been an unqualified success.

The alternative solution, located by the National Gallery's scientific adviser, Ian Rawlins, in September 1940, turned out to be the Manod quarry at Blaenau Ffestiniog in north Wales. Protected by 200 feet of rock, and with access by a tunnel, it had essential services connected to it, but would need massive conversion before it could provide the right environment for irreplaceable masterpieces. Building work began, and between August and September 1941 the entire National Gallery collection was moved to the quarry.

The Blitz

While Rawlins was reconnoitring locations, the bombs were falling on London and other cities. G P Jooste, a young South African diplomat, vividly described the night of 10 September 1941.

The night was in every respect unforgettable, worrying yet spectacular. Literally thousands of fire bombs were dropped on the city until it seemed inevitable that this world city would die in flames. On the roof of South Africa House where it was no more dangerous than inside the building we watched this destruction with a feeling of astonishment; a destruction, it appeared, not only of a metropolis but also of so much that commemorated Britain's history and of so much that its fame was based on.

Ten days later, a bomb fell between South Africa House and St Martin-in-the-Fields but did remarkably little damage. By contrast, 12 October was a bad night for the Square. A 250-kilogram high-explosive bomb hit the National Gallery and destroyed what is now Room 10; infinitely worse, another landed close to Trafalgar Square Underground station and penetrated into the ticket hall where it exploded, injuring 33 people and killing seven: Sigvart and Brandal Petersen from Norway, Violet Hancock, Alice and John Johns, Pauline Smith and Hilda Woodward. Earlier in the month a crowd of about 2000 had listened to speakers, including the redoubtable Dr Edith Summerskill, appealing for equal air-raid injury compensation for men and women.

The bomb that landed in one of the National Gallery's courtyards on 17 October failed to detonate and the Royal Engineers were called in to defuse it. Fortunately, when it did explode six days later, the bomb squad had gone off to lunch and the only casualty was the architecture.

Canada House likewise watched the Blitz with anxiety. The Canadian Military Headquarters was next door to the High Commission, in the Canada Sun Life Assurance building, and it suffered both bomb damage and minor casualties to its personnel. Major C P Stacey reported:

On the morning of 7 Nov. there was a hit on the Royal College of Physicians and Surgeons on the north-east corner of the block, but fortunately the damage was limited. On the night of

Priceless paintings are for the second time loaded into a van, this time bound for the Manod quarry to safeguard them from Nazi air attack.

A traction engine is brought in to remove heavy debris left by the German bomb that exploded close to the statue of Charles I and caused seven deaths. In the background, the base of Nelson's Column is covered with a morale-boosting banner.

14–15 Nov., the well-known furniture store, Hamptons Limited, in Pall Mall East between the National Gallery and Whitcomb Street, immediately across the street from the College of Physicians and Surgeons and the Sun Life Building, was struck and burned out; the remains of this building have now been demolished.

First Secretary Lester B Pearson, later to be one of his country's finest prime ministers, reported to Ottawa:

So far Canada House has been fortunate. We have had two high explosive bombs – both at night – so near that it is surprising they did not shatter parts of the building. But they have only smashed some of our windows and thrown part of the road on the roof! One bomb landed on the pavement behind the Sun Life. It was a large one, made a big crater and broke the water main so that our shelter…was soon flooded. This occurred in the middle of the night and caused some of the senior officers at Military headquarters…to leave in a manner…characterised more by speed than dignity. …The other close bomb landed about 20 yards in front of my window, between Canada House and the Canadian Pacific building… It appears, however, that it went down very deep and exploded in such a way that the blast was almost entirely underground. We are not complaining about that! In addition there is also a bomb crater further down by Nelson's column, and the other morning we were rather surprised when, out of a blue sky, a heavy one went off just by the National Gallery.

A bomb exploding somewhere near Villiers Street blew out the altar windows of St Martin's, and shortly afterwards the vicar died, probably from heart failure brought on by shock. Like the South Africans and the Canadians, the staff of St Martin's posted fire watchers on the roof of their building and to pass the time they formed a singing group. This was the genesis of the St Martin's Singers, a choir that is still going strong.

The National Gallery might have evacuated its paintings and turned itself into a café, the profits of which went to charity, but, largely thanks to the determination of its Director, Kenneth, later Lord, Clark it was soon back in the business of exhibiting. Modern British art and paintings by war artists drew in thousands of visitors. In 1941, the publicly expressed wish of Sir Charles Wheeler to see a newly acquired Rembrandt led directly to the 'Picture of the Month' whereby every month one of the Gallery's collection was brought back and put on display for three weeks. Equally uplifting for music lovers were the weekly lunchtime concerts at the gallery initiated by the pianist, Dame Myra Hess.

At the start of the war, staff at the Sun Insurance office next to Canadian Pacific were told to start work promptly at 9.45 a.m. and to leave no later than 6 p.m. When the danger became more acute, staff were evacuated to Leatherhead leaving just two employees to hold the fort. A blast in April 1941 damaged the premises, which were repaired after 1945.

Westminster Archives possesses a very large-scale map of the city on which every recorded bomb or rocket incident is plotted by hand and cross-referenced to the report files. Looking at the colour-coded spots around the perimeter of Trafalgar Square it seems little short of a miracle that out of the 30,000 or so Londoners killed by aerial attack only eight people lost their lives there; that the damage to the buildings was, comparatively speaking, so light; and that the only monument to be damaged was one of the lions. The terrible blast at the Underground station mangled its forelegs.

Peace and reconstruction

At 3 p.m. on 8 May 1945 Prime Minister Winston Churchill broadcast to the nation that the war in Europe was officially over – although thousands of Allied troops were still engaged out in the Far East – but the news had already leaked out. After some five years of bombs, rockets and rationing, London could at last celebrate.

Vast crowds, many sporting red-white-and-blue, came out on to the streets, packing Trafalgar Square until even the lions were covered with jubilant revellers. Huge loudspeakers relayed the King's address from Buckingham Palace. Celebrations continued into the night, and long after the last trains had left, those same revellers were walking home, sore-footed but elated and, above all, relieved.

Throughout the war, London had been a heavily defended no-fly zone for all aircraft. Even in early May 1945 Captain Lou Tilley of the US Airforce was used to making a great swing westwards round it when flying between France and his base in East Anglia, but when his navigator, Bill Rellstab, picked up the news of the German surrender on Forces' Radio, Tilley asked for a course for London: the temptation to be the first plane to buzz London was irresistible. From the Plexiglas nose of the Flying Fortress, Rellstab looked down and saw:

…the scene of a lifetime. There were hundreds of thousands of people. It looked like millions…they were swarming over the statues in Trafalgar Square and Piccadilly Circus. Some were waving flags and banners and articles of clothing. It was as if you had kicked off the top of a huge anthill. I could see their faces. They were all turned up towards us and they were shouting and laughing and waving their arms wildly at us, and I was smiling and waving back. What a way to end the war!

With the signing of the final peace the country could begin the long haul back towards a new normality. Many of the armed forces were still away on active service; cities such as Liverpool and Plymouth shared the London cityscape of shattered buildings and jagged bomb craters; the civilian population continued to queue with ration books. And although there could be said to be more pressing needs in the capital, it was surely a matter of pride to restore symbolic places to their former glory.

The National Gallery took a lead by bringing home the first paintings within days of the end of the war. The air-raid shelter in the Square was taken down and repairs made to the paving. A 1940 inspection of Nelson by steeplejack Sid Larkins had revealed a slight gap between the two halves of his body, and this was made good with mastic in 1946. The lion that had been blasted out of position was reinstated by Mowlem, who were on site at the time, but the remoulding of the fractured forelegs was delayed until 1950 when the contract was given to the Fiorini Art Bronze Foundry at Fulham. The Office of Works resumed the task of completing the memorial fountains.

Abies picea

Before they were finished, the Norwegians provided a burst of Christmas cheer with the gift of a Christmas tree. The tall Norway spruce, *Abies picea*, was given by the Travel Association of Norway to promote links between the two countries and as a

'thank you' for Britain's assistance during the war. The Norwegian Government in exile had met in London; support had been given to the country's Resistance; broadcasts in Norwegian had helped to keep up morale; and King Haakon VII had found a warm welcome in Britain after his escape from occupied Norway. A popular gift developed into a tradition maintained by the city of Oslo.

The Norwegians take justifiable pride in the selection, care and felling of a specimen which, as they say themselves, is probably the most famous Christmas tree in the world. The traditional switching on of the lights on the first Thursday of December in London is preceded by an equally traditional felling ceremony outside Oslo. Schoolchildren from Norway and abroad sing carols, coffee and sandwiches are served in the forest, and the whole proceeding is carried out in the presence of the Lord Mayor of Westminster, the British Ambassador and the Mayor of Oslo. DFDS Tor Line provides free shipping, and even the crew to bring the tree to London is specially chosen.

Nothing in Trafalgar Square passes unnoticed; even the Christmas tree has found itself at the centre of a protest over acid rain caused by pollution from British power stations that falls on Norway. Police in both countries were put on a tree-kidnap alert after Natur og Ungdom, a Norwegian environmental group, threatened to sabotage the 1985 gift to make the point that acid rain was destroying the forests in which the trees were grown. Two years later, firemen using a turntable ladder were called to remove two Norwegian protestors who climbed the tree shortly before the lighting ceremony and unveiled a 'Stop Acid Rain' banner.

Unveiling the new-look Square

The 1947 tree was set up against a background of dismantled fountains. The following year would be a different story. Appropriately enough on Trafalgar Day, the Duke of Gloucester unveiled the busts of Beatty and Jellicoe which had been placed against the north wall (Jellicoe to the right of Nelson as befitting

OPPOSITE VE Day brought thousands into the Square including this ecstatic group of young women from the Women's Royal Naval Service. Throughout the war women had performed vital and often highly skilled work, frequently in vulnerable locations. Some had filled the traditional roles, but others had taken on new roles, including mechanics, decoders, book-keepers, signal interceptors and translators.

The Norwegian Christmas tree, seen here at the first lighting ceremony in 1947 rapidly became an indispensable part of Christmas celebrations in London. The lights, always white to recreate the effect of candles, were run on electricity until 2004 when a hydrogen fuel cell was used, making that tree the greenest ever. Note the fountains, the remodelling of which is still incomplete.

his senior rank) and officially inaugurated the new fountains. Gone were the steam engines. Beneath the south-eastern corner of the Square lay a new pumping station and control room with three electric pumps to serve the different features, from the great central jets, capable of sending the water at least 80 feet into the air, to the Prince-of-Wales feathers, the cascade and the bronzes. A great deal of experimentation had gone into the arrangements, including trials with fire jets. The basins were lined with blue tiles to brighten the water and steel conduits in the pavement allowed for floodlighting in four colours, with a 30-second fade facility as required. Additional conduits were laid which could carry the BBC's amplification equipment.

Another new feature to be added was the flowerbeds along the wall. The Office of Works had flirted with the idea of injecting some colour in 1938 when they had considered licensing flower stalls or women with baskets of flowers for sale. Both suggestions were rejected on the grounds that they would set awkward precedents and generate no rents, and also because 'Costermongers and other street traders are rather a difficult class to deal with and control. Their appearance, language and general behaviour often leaves much to be desired'. However, after the war flowerbeds were temporarily installed and proved almost too popular, especially at lunchtime. The man in charge of the Square wrote to the Office in 1949:

> The ledges of the raised beds have proved a boon to the weary and I recently counted some ninety-seven citizens resting from their labours upon them. It so happens that the ledges are exactly the right height to support the human form…they put their coats and lunches upon the flowers.

Later he had even less sympathy for the picnicking citizens whose behaviour 'nullifies our attempts to decorate the area horticulturally and makes a mockery of the design and layout'.

One suggestion that failed was a 1949 proposal by Admiral Holland, Chairman of King George's Fund for Sailors, for a war memorial for all seafarers, naval and merchant, from the whole of the Commonwealth. He had in mind a frieze along the north wall showing various classes of naval, merchant and fishing vessels with an inscription where wreaths could be laid. The National Union of Seamen and the First Sea Lord supported it, but the idea was dropped when it failed to secure the backing of the National Maritime Board and ship owners: the latter group felt that the public would equate it only with the Royal Navy and the money could, in any case, be better spent on practical help.

The coronation of Queen Elizabeth II

Eight years on from VE Day and the jubilant crowds, estimated at over a million, were out for the Queen's coronation on 2 June 1953. Many had camped overnight, some for longer, along the route.

The weather was cool and wet, but just for a moment, as the gilded state coach approached Trafalgar Square on its way to Westminster Abbey, the sun achieved a faint smile. Then the rain became heavy, soaking all those listening to the service as it was broadcast through loudspeakers from the Abbey. Household Cavalryman, John Hardy, vividly remembered the effect on the white sap used on their uniforms:

> It ran on to jackets, pockets were lined with white paste,
> the white sap from our breeches settled on to the black
> sheepskins covering our saddles and ran down boots.
> Uniforms had to be chucked away at the end of the day,
> absolutely ruined,

That night, from the balcony of Buckingham Palace the Queen switched on a lighting display that flowed from the Mall as far as the Tower of London. Admiralty Arch and the National Gallery blazed into life and the fountains in the Square ran silver.

OPPOSITE The ceremony at which the memorials to Admirals Jellicoe and Beatty were unveiled was organised with military precision. The two portrait busts can be seen towards the middle of the north wall where they remained until the recent construction of the central staircase. The flowerbeds are also in place.

LEFT Crowds defy the rain to watch the 1953 coronation procession, hoping for a glimpse of the young Queen whose state coach can be seen turning into Mall Approach. Drummond's Bank stands on the corner with Whitehall. Opposite, the Malaya and Singapore High Commission staff and guests watch from their grandstand.

Nelson's Column rises from a sea of faces protesting in 1967 against the nuclear arms race at a demonstration organised by CND. The fear of a nuclear war between the USSR and USA was ever present; in 1961 the Cuban Missile Crisis had the world holding its breath.

Photographers and journalists jostle around actress Vanessa Redgrave as she addresses a crowd of around 15,000 at a demonstration against the Vietnam War on 17 March 1968. Wearing a headband, a Vietnamese symbol of mourning she explained, she marched with the crowd to the US Embassy at Grosvenor Square, where protestors clashed with the police.

The CND protests

The Second World War had ended with the dropping of the atomic bomb; during the ensuing decades of the Cold War an increasing number of those nations with nuclear capability engaged in rounds of tests. In 1951 – the year that saw Trafalgar Square officially proclaimed as the centre of London by the Department of Transport (all distances from London are measured from the statue of Charles I) – the staff of the Civil Defence Staff College and the Scientific Adviser's Branch listened to a paper hypothesising the aftermath of a nuclear bomb exploding above Nelson's Column. Perhaps unsurprisingly, the first great protest campaign of the post-war years began in 1958 with the Campaign for Nuclear Disarmament's (CND) first march. Watching the rounds of nuclear

tests in the context of the Cold War, its adherents feared a Third World War fought with nuclear weapons; CND's opponents regarded nuclear weapons as the ultimate deterrent. CND drew its supporters from pacifists, students, environmentalists and the Church and attracted high-profile names from politics, science and the media, largely on the political left. In the absence of any serious moves towards multilateral disarmament, CND campaigned peacefully for a unilateral move by Britain.

As the site of the Atomic Weapons Establishment, Aldermaston was the target of many of the early protests which took the form of large marches either from Trafalgar Square to Aldermaston or vice versa. Support waxed and waned: protests against the Vietnam War in the 1960s drew attention away from matters nuclear; the

arrival of US missiles in the 1980s revived the cause but shifted the focus away from Aldermaston to Greenham Common.

Uganda House

A third High Commission arrived on the Square at the end of the decade with the construction of Uganda House at the junction of Cockspur Street and Mall Approach. The building, technically 58–59 Trafalgar Square, is relatively inconspicuous and blends into the general grey architecture of the area.

Excavations on the site for Uganda House brought to light the fossilised remains of animals including hippo, elephant and a large ox. This was neither the first nor the last time that such ostensibly incongruous discoveries were made around the Square: during the rebuilding of Drummond's in the late 1870s the bones of lion, elephant and hippo were found at a depth of 29 feet. Scientists from various disciplines have been able to build up a fascinating picture of London during the Ice Age. We now know that the ice sheet stopped as it reached Finsbury Park, and reindeer, lions, woolly mammoths and aurochs roamed freely on land now covered by office blocks, hotels, art galleries, theatres and roads.

At the same time as Uganda House was opening, a dispute was brewing over plans to remove the recently installed but, paradoxically, second oldest statue on the Square – James II in the costume of a Roman emperor. Eleven years earlier, in 1947, the Chelsea Society had vociferously but in vain opposed the relocation of the King, easily one of England's least favourite monarchs, from Whitehall to the grass terrace of the National Gallery. Now that latter institution and the RFAC were equally passionate, and ultimately successful, about keeping him. Their argument was simple: the sculptor was Grinling Gibbons (1648–1721) and the statue, cast in 1686, could fairly claim to be one of the capital's finest outdoor bronzes. The statue intended to replace James was William MacMillan's newly commissioned Sir Walter Raleigh which, in the end, went to Whitehall Gardens.

Canada expands

The Royal College of Physicians was by far the oldest resident on the Square, but the time had come to move on. They had commissioned a building at Regent's Park, which gained immediate Grade I conservation status, designed as it was not just for their practical needs but also to do justice to their history and to accommodate the Library and the Censor's Room, both of which, as with previous moves, would accompany them.

Their departure allowed the Canadian High Commission to expand laterally, and in 1965 a major development programme was put into place. Although Sir Robert Smirke appeared to have constructed a single building, in reality the floors did not correspond and the two halves of the building had to be connected. The plans, which included removing one of the staircases and changing some of the panelled rooms left behind by the College, caused anxiety among British conservationists during a decade in which the country as a whole saw too many good buildings bulldozed or altered beyond recognition. Westminster Council and the RFAC were brought into the controversy, and there were calls for a preservation order to halt the works. The new owners felt that too many of their critics had spoken without even seeing the interior of Smirke's building, and at a meeting inside the High Commission an amicable compromise was worked out that allowed for modified immediate changes and the possibility of future restoration if required. A much more sympathetic refurbishment, unveiled by the Queen in 1998, recreated some of the features that had been taken out in previous years and uncovered others which had been hidden by false ceilings.

Once permission had been granted, tales began to circulate, including rumours of ghosts and pickled specimens. One persistent rumour is of secret tunnels, now bricked up, leading from the basement, possibly a legacy of the war years when Canadian Military Headquarters was in close contact with the War Office. The plans do show basement vaults, some of which were bricked

ABOVE The Queen and Canadian Premier, Jean Chretien, leave Canada House after the 1998 re-opening ceremony. The major refurbishment and restoration had brought to light many of the original features hidden in the 1960s.

OPPOSITE In 1961 Drummond's Bank opened the country's first drive-through bank. Discreetly concealed behind the shrubbery, it had to be wide enough to accommodate the Rolls Royce and other types of luxury car driven by its clientele.

General Eisenhower said of Cunningham: 'He was the Nelsonian type of admiral. He believed that ships went to sea in order to find and destroy the enemy. He thought always in terms of attack, never of defence. He was vigorous, hardy, intelligent and straightforward. In spite of the toughness, the degree of affection in which he was held by all grades and ranks of the British navy...was nothing short of remarkable. He was a real sea dog'.

ABC in the Square

If Nelson could have chosen the men with whom to share Trafalgar Square, he would surely have picked the admiral whose statue by the outstanding Czech sculptor, Franta Belsky (1921–2000), which stands against the north wall, was unveiled by the Duke of Edinburgh on 2 April 1967. Andrew Browne Cunningham, later Viscount Hyndehope (1883–1963), known as ABC from his initials, was indisputably the most successful British naval commander of the twentieth century and perhaps the only one since Nelson to warrant true comparison with the great man. He achieved some fame as a resourceful destroyer captain during the First World War but it was his actions during the Second, as Admiral-in-Command of the Mediterranean Fleet, that assured his reputation.

At the Battle of Matapan in March 1941 he demonstrated his maxim that 'the only place at which it is proper for naval ships to fire at the enemy is at point blank range' by leading his fleet to sink three Italian cruisers and two destroyers. In true Nelsonian tradition, he had ignored the rulebook for night engagements against an unknown foe by sailing towards the enemy, achieving total surprise. The battle was of huge significance in keeping the Italians in their harbours and away from critical operations in Greece and Crete. It was a great morale boost for Britain in a dark period of the war nearly 18 months before El Alamein.

Cunningham's personal contribution to ultimate victory was as great as any, being responsible for the naval forces supplying to Malta and Tobruk and the evacuation of Greece. When personally committing the fleet, which was suffering great losses at the time, to the complete the evacuation of British troops from Crete, he told the other military chiefs in Cairo: 'it takes three years to build a ship but three hundred years to build a tradition'. Out of 22,000 troops on Crete 16,500 were rescued, but at the cost of 3 cruisers and 6 destroyers sunk and a further 15 major warships damaged.

In 1942, he was second-in-command to General Dwight Eisenhower in the Mediterranean theatre of war and was

up around 1925, and there was, in particular, a small passage and stairs leading down to the Union Club's beer store.

Contrary to what many non-Canadians believe, Canada House is no longer the High Commission. Since 1971 the latter has been housed at Grosvenor Square, and although official functions are still held there, Canada House has taken on the role of an information and cultural centre: a focal point for expatriates and Canadian tourists and the venue for events and exhibitions of Canadian art. As a nation, Canada has made few international enemies: possibly the only anti-Canadian demonstrations to take place outside in the Square have been against the seal hunt.

In 1906, General Election results had been projected in Trafalgar Square using a 'magic lantern', the forerunner of the slide projector. By 1970 the 'big screen' was here to stay, allowing crowds to gather and share the unfolding drama across the country.

responsible for the amphibious landings by Allied troops invading North Africa, Sicily and Italy. Later the following year, he became Admiral of the Fleet and First Sea Lord, responsible for the overall strategic direction of the navy for the remainder of the war, a period including the Normandy landings and British fleet operations in the Pacific. As a member of the Chiefs of Staff committee he was present with Churchill at the great conferences at Yalta and Potsdam. He retired in 1946.

One of his diary reminiscences was of looking out over London from the Admiralty during the victory celebrations and noticing with satisfaction that the only statue he could see illuminated was that of Nelson in Trafalgar Square.

Social care at St Martin-in-the-Fields

With the end of the war, the crypt of St Martin's had ceased to play such a major role in the life of the Square. It was used for the vicar's Shrove Tuesday party and at Christmas the Salvation Army band played there. Christmas dinner followed by entertainment, tea and a parting present were provided for the homeless and poor of the parish, in three sittings. The logistics of rotating the guests, many of whom turned up without tickets, began to prove so difficult that in 1966 the event was changed into a buffet in the crypt. Eight hundred people turned up for food, warmth and a packet of cigarettes. It was a sign to the Church to reach out in new ways to the disadvantaged.

Clients from The Connection at St Martin's, with one of the security staff, pause on the famous steps of the church for a photograph with the vicar, the Reverend Nicholas Holtam. Thousands of people have been helped by the church's 'practical and hospitable Christianity that cares for those in need'.

The issue of homelessness was not as high on the political agenda as it is now. There were many people living alone in the substandard accommodation offered by the city's hostels and boarding houses, and while the closing of such hostels increased the homeless figures, it was also true that people disliked being institutionalised and felt demeaned by having to live in dormitories. In 1966 St Martin's set up a Sunday soup kitchen which ran for 30 years, but there was a growing realisation that things had to be done better; services had to be more personal even if that meant helping fewer. And it was no longer a matter of giving purely physical help: substance abuse and loneliness were recognised as real issues.

It was at this time that Cecil King, proprietor of the *Daily Mirror* and friend of Austen Williams, Vicar of St Martin's, visited Australia to observe how that country was dealing with similar problems. On his return, he gave a grant to St Martin's which allowed them to extend their services and staffing. As part of the new service they set up a hostel in Clapham, which offered individual rooms rather than dormitories; recently it was rebuilt to double the accommodation. Open-Line, a telephone help-line, offered advice and a friendly ear; it ceased only when new players such as local radio stations came into the field.

The Social Care Unit, which was established in 1948, opened a daycentre in the vaults in 1980. The location was not ideal: the vaults were old and too cramped to accommodate the expanding services. As well as providing cheap meals and advice on finding housing, the Unit offered basic medical services including chiropody. Eventually, skills such as computer studies, creative writing, music and art groups were included in the programme to allow clients to explore their creativity, gain self-respect and find an identity that was not defined by homelessness.

When the old school building to the north of the church became vacant in the 1980s it was turned into a club for young people visiting London, but when it became apparent that those who used it had even more pressing needs a programme was set up for them. In 1989 the Centre at St Martin's combined with the Soho Project drug agency and St James's café – based at St James's Piccadilly – to establish the London Connection in order to co-ordinate services for all disadvantaged young people.

The winter of 1986–7 was savagely cold. The probability of a high number of deaths from hypothermia among rough sleepers brought appeals for help from charities such as Crisis at Christmas. St James's church opened its doors and St Martin's set up an overnight soup kitchen staffed by the many volunteers who came forward. It was a turning point, and local authorities began to support agencies such as the London Connection and the Social Care Unit in tackling the rough sleeping epidemic among young and old alike. In 2003 the two organisations decided to coordinate their work under the title of The Connection at St Martin's.

The monstrous carbuncle

By the late 1970s, and despite another relatively recent addition to the north, the National Gallery's need to expand became urgent again and it was decided to develop the former Hampton's furniture store site, purchased much earlier by the government. The 'catch' was the incorporation of commercial office space below the exhibition rooms. A competition was held, leading to the choice of Ahrends Burton and Koralek in 1982.

First, a public enquiry demanded modifications to the plans; then, in May 1984, the Prince of Wales stood up to make a speech to the Royal Institute of British Architects (RIBA) at its 150th Anniversary Dinner. It was the second bomb to be dropped on the site and possibly only the second compliment for William Wilkins' original building.

Instead of designing an extension to the elegant façade of the National Gallery, which complements it and continues the

For decades, Hampton & Sons, here depicted in its 1870 Almanac, had retailed carpets, furniture and soft furnishings from its Pall Mall East premises opposite Canada House. All that ended with a high-explosive bomb in 1941, and the site remained empty, earmarked for a possible expansion of the National Gallery next door.

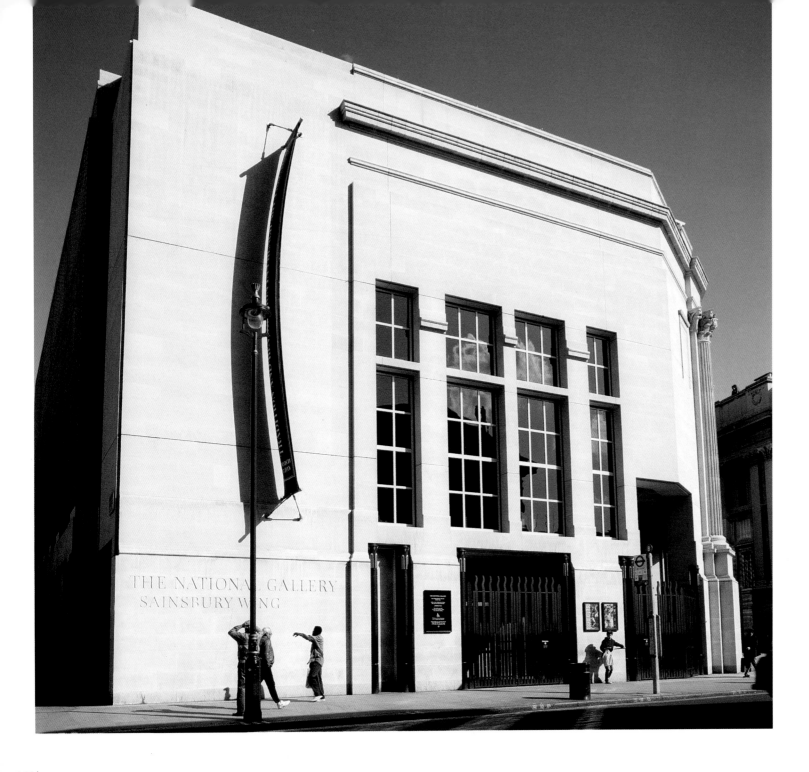

concept of columns and domes, we may be presented with a kind of municipal fire station, complete with the sort of tower that contains the siren…a monstrous carbuncle on the face of a much-loved and elegant friend.

The speech ultimately benefited the National Gallery. The Secretary of State refused permission for the extension and the architects withdrew. Sir John, now Lord, Sainsbury and his brothers stepped forward with an offer to fund a building exclusively for the National Gallery.

The new commission went to an American architect, Robert Venturi, of Venturi Scott Brown and the Sainsbury Wing opened in 1991. While modern and asymmetrical, the façade continued the theme of the original through Corinthian pilasters and the obligatory Portland stone, but it combined the traditional material with modern black glass.

The Sainsbury Wing was designed specifically for the Early Renaissance works by artists including Pisanello, Van Eyck, the Bellinis, Campin and Botticelli. Just as the Renaissance artists revelled in perspective, so Venturi Scott Brown played with perspective to tease the visitors. The great granite staircase leading to the exhibition rooms is broader at the top than at the bottom, making the climb seem rather less than it is; columns cunningly appear to frame a painting.

Equally important are the technical features which provide carefully controlled light, heat and humidity for these demanding tenants, the oldest and arguably the most fragile in the Gallery. Visitors are sometimes startled when, just as they stand rapt in contemplation, the lights go down and they have to wait for a moment before resuming their admiration.

Grand Buildings

The Prince's speech to RIBA probably played its part in saving Trafalgar Square from a potential second carbuncle. Having spoken of his disappointment with the ultimately doomed Ahrends' plans for the National Gallery, he turned to the second proposed redevelopment.

As if the National Gallery extension wasn't enough they are now apparently planning to redevelop the large, oval-bellied nineteenth-century building, known as the Grand Hotel, which stands on the south-west corner of Trafalgar Square and which was saved from demolition in 1974 after a campaign to rescue it. As with the National Gallery, I believe the plan is to put this redevelopment out to competition, in which case we can only criticise the judges and not the architects, for I suspect there will be some entries representative of the present-day school of Romantic Pragmatism, which could at least provide an alternative.

There were, and the commission went to one of them.

Siddell, Gibson and Associates, whose design was chosen largely on the merits of the interior planning, opted to build a virtual replica of the original exterior, and the 27,000 Portland and Bath stones that were cut to clad the entire building made Grand Buildings the largest single masonry contract placed for half a century. Bramante's renaissance courtyard at the Vatican was the model for the ground level arcade that shelters pedestrians and hides the modern shop fronts, and bas reliefs of endangered species by the sculptor Barry Baldwin decorate the façade. Inside, however, Renaissance Italy meets turn-of-the-millennium London in a seven-floor atrium.

Anti-apatheid

For 30 years the cause most closely identified with Trafalgar Square was the anti-apartheid movement. The election of the National Party in 1948 in South Africa had been followed by the introduction of apartheid laws to segregate racial groups, and 11

OPPOSITE *The ground floor of the Sainsbury Wing houses the gift shop and information desk and is a popular place for visitors to meet up. The first floor includes conference rooms, a restaurant and a computer information suite for the public, while the top floor, linked to the main building, is divided into 16 rooms which provide 2053 square metres of wall space for the exhibition of the Early Renaissance Collection of Italian and Northern paintings.*

On the far left, the stone façade of the new renaissance-inspired Grand Buildings glows warmly; on the other side of the road, 1 Northumberland Avenue, now a refurbished office block, turns the corner between that street and Whitehall, losing much of its rich colour in the sunlight. To the right of Nelson's Column, Drummond's Bank guards one side of the entrance to Admiralty Arch, while 58–59 Trafalgar Square, better known as Uganda House, stands sentinel on the other. Dating from 1865 and originally built for £20,000, 60–61, the former Sun Insurance office abutting it was occupied by the world's oldest insurance company from 1866 until 1975. The blazing sun logo has gone from the façade. The frieze of its neighbour, 62–65, which is floodlit at night, proclaims the name of Canadian Pacific, but the famous shipping company moved out in 2004 after a century. Following some years as a steak house, William Potter's ornate Union Bank building of 1872, number 66 and just showing on the far right of the photograph, underwent a complete internal makeover in 2004 to become Albannach, a Scottish-themed bar and restaurant.

years later South African exiles and their UK supporters began a campaign in Britain against the resulting oppression, starting with a call for a boycott of South African goods. The presence of the South Africa High Commission in such a prominent location offered protesters the perfect location for large, media-grabbing protests, all the more so after the convictions for treason of African National Congress (ANC) leaders including Nelson Mandela in 1962–3.

Demonstrations, sit-downs and vigils continued almost annually alongside other tactics. Later, the ANC and its supporters, many of them drawn from the media, entertainment, politics and various faiths, succeeded in equating the call for majority rule in South Africa with their demand for Mandela's freedom, giving a sharpened focus to the rallies. His release in 1990 symbolised the beginning of the end of apartheid; four years later the crowds were cheering universal suffrage in South Africa, and since then the once-vilified High Commission has become a place of celebration.

The building, however, posed a challenge to post-apartheid diplomats, containing as it did many artistic features that ranged from patronising to deeply offensive. Because South Africa House is a Listed Building, any changes had to be acceptable to statutory bodies such as English Heritage and the Crown Agents.

Refurbishment Manager and Consultant, Lorna de Smidt, worked closely with architect, Glen Robinson, and decided that they needed,

> …to change the ambience of the interior. We were
> determined to shift away from the 'nod and wink' that the
> apartheid government of the 1980s had offered to the
> presence of indigenous people in South Africa: all rather tacky
> bits of beadwork, woven baskets and such like. The best way
> to deal with the murals, friezes and paintings was to
> contextualise them.

One of the most distasteful murals depicts a scene where the then Governor-General of the Cape, Simon van der Stel, accepts gifts of copper from crouching, subservient indigenous people. Another is a scene on the farm owned by his brother, Willem van der Stel, depicting white-aproned slaves looking deliriously happy while harvesting an unidentifiable crop. To set these in context, Sue Williamson has been commissioned to etch on glass four pages from van der Stel's diary which give the names of his slaves, where in the Dutch East Indies they came from, how old they were, what he paid for them. 'In this way', said Ms de Smidt, 'we would be able to retain this nasty work but put another historical slant to it. And the fact that it is also bad art will be neither here nor there'.

The landscapes by Hendrik Pierneef were all of high quality and, except that they raise the sensitive question of land ownership, are largely uncontroversial. Only one Pierneef shows intervention: a landscape with the tiniest of human (black) figures. Clear glass etched with writing has been placed over it, allowing an unimpeded view. When, however, a light is switched on the text of the African National Congress Freedom Charter is shadowed on to the landscape, the only overtly political statement.

Two new artists, Sandile Zulu and Willem Boshoff, have received commissions. As Lorna de Smidt explains:

> When the new democratic government took charge of South
> Africa House, there was not one painting by a black artist. We
> decided that there are a sufficient number of black artists of
> international stature who could be approached to come up
> with ideas for making the building reflect the demographic
> reality of the country. But we were also not prepared to ignore
> the white artists who could also make a contribution. We
> were not going to take our cue from the ideological detritus
> left behind by the apartheid regime.

OPPOSITE Some of the country's best-loved actors threw their weight behind the anti-apartheid struggle. In October 1976 Sheila Hancock, Albert Finney, Robert Morley, Kenneth Haigh and the irrepressible Kenneth Williams joined protestors outside South Africa House to call for the release of John Kani and Winston Ntshona.

RIGHT A lone anti-apartheid protester in 1960 urges people to support the call not to buy South African goods and produce.

The solution, extended to other murals and friezes, was nothing if not imaginative.

Poll tax riot

The events of 1990 kept the media spotlight on Trafalgar Square. On the positive side, there were celebrations following the release of Mandela, a plea from the Trustees of the National Gallery for the pedestrianisation of the north side of the Square and the opening of two handsome new buildings, the Sainsbury Wing and Grand Buildings; these were contrasted against the worst violence seen on the Square, certainly for a century. The cause was opposition to the Community Charge – popularly called the poll tax – which had just been introduced by Prime Minister Margaret Thatcher's government as a means of collecting local taxes. Even with concessions to the poorest, it was widely felt to transfer the tax burden to the less well off, and the Trafalgar Square demonstration was the culmination of months of vociferous local protests and refusals to pay.

Organisers of the massive march from Downing Street to Trafalgar Square in the brilliant sunshine of 31 March had hoped for a peaceful protest with demonstrators gathering to listen to speakers in the Square, but trouble began near the start and

escalated into a riot on the Square which lasted into the night and involved around 3000 of the huge crowd. Stewards vainly tried to calm the situation as protestors smashed windows to loot shops on the south side, and mounted police launched charges in which at least one woman went down.

Rioters wrecked the gates to the almost completed Grand Buildings and swarmed up the scaffolding to encourage fellow rioters. Scaffolding poles from the site were added to bottles and stones hurled by the crowd, and arson caused thousand of pounds worth of damage to the almost completed building and its equipment. A passing motorist was dragged from his car to which the rioters then set fire.

When dispersed from the Square, the violent minority ran up St Martin's Lane towards theatre-land, smashing windows, raiding shops and setting fire to cars as they went. Over 300 arrests were made and more than 100 police and civilians sustained injuries; as soon as the trouble ended, claims and counterclaims of unprovoked violence began.

Ultimately, opposition to the poll tax led to the Prime Minister's resignation, and the tax was repealed by John Major's government.

The fourth plinth

The two plinths built into the northern corners of the Square had been intended for statues of monarchs, but only George IV succeeded in obtaining a place, and the fourth plinth, as it has become known, has remained empty since Sir Charles Barry first laid out the Square. Originally it was anticipated that the plinth would be occupied by an equestrian statue of William IV, but for financial reasons one was not commissioned. Many of the people who might, in earlier decades, have laid claim to it have been commemorated with statues elsewhere, and the question of what to do with the empty pedestal has become a vexed one for a generation encouraged to feel ill at ease with its past, particularly so when it comes to military leaders. The overriding fear has to be

that anyone chosen now for such a significant position must be able to stand the test of time: no embarrassing skeletons from public or private life must lurk in the cupboard, and the choice must be acceptable to a majority within each ethnic, religious and gender grouping. Such paragons, if they even exist, are few.

In 1985 The Royal Society of Arts (RSA) asked for nominations from members of the public, and received some surprising suggestions, including Winnie the Pooh. The committee was to reach the conclusion that Trafalgar Square was simply so famous that nobody could agree what should be done about the plinth. The solution to the problem is ongoing: the temporary exhibition of modern works of sculpture began with Mark Wallinger's statue of Christ: *Ecce Homo: Behold the Man*. The works have proved, as expected and intended, controversial, but those who dislike one particular piece have the consolation of knowing it is not a permanent feature, and those who deride the whole process can enjoy periods of respite when the plinth is empty.

As the twentieth century and the previous millennium drew to a close, eyes turned away from the centre of London and fastened on the Millennium Dome where so many of the problems and controversies surrounding the creation of Trafalgar Square were replayed over a mercifully shorter length of time. But the older site had not been forgotten. For six months of 1997, architect Sir Norman Foster was drawing up plans for major changes to a Square, for too long a giant, pigeon-infested roundabout which came alive only at Christmas and New Year or whenever there were enough demonstrators to lay claim to it. The Foster recommendations for both Trafalgar and Parliament Squares were published under the ambitious title of 'World Squares For All'.

In August 1998 the Deputy Prime Minister, John Prescott, announced that the £50 million plan would be implemented. There was, he said, 'overwhelming public support for turning these historic squares from being giant traffic islands into places where people can relax and enjoy the sights at the heart of our capital'.

Bill Woodrow's sculpture, Regardless of History, *that occupied the fourth plinth in 2000, deals with man's inability to learn the lessons of the past. 'The large head has fallen and is resting on its side on top of the plinth under the weight of the book, and the two components are kept and locked in place on the plinth by the massive root system of a tree that has taken seed and grown on top of the sculpture… Together with the head and book [the tree] makes reference to the never-ending cyclical relationship between civilisations, knowledge and the forces of nature'.*

CHAPTER 6   INTO THE MILLENNIUM

Pedestrians first

The Foster plan had the virtue of simplicity, and the only losers were to be the motorists whose cars crawled painfully from one set of traffic lights to the next. It also dovetailed neatly with plans by both the government and the Mayor of London to reduce the number of vehicles entering Central London, which overcame initial fears that congestion in the area might be made worse. Almost everyone, from English Heritage to Westminster City Council was in favour, and the implementation of the scheme, costed at £25 million for Trafalgar Square, went ahead with a fluency rare in the Square's history.

Between the granting of planning permission in 2001 and the commencement of work the following year posters and leaflets warned motorists of the changes ahead. The road between the National Gallery and the terrace was closed to traffic from 1 September and initial delays for confused motorists brought the expected crop of complaints. Visitors, however, were for the first time able to reach the National and the Portrait Galleries from the Square – and, by extension, from the Underground, without having to go to the traffic lights or risk crossing unaided.

Both Sir Charles Barry and William Wilkins had wanted a broad staircase leading up to the terrace, and Foster's plans realised their vision. At the end of October the granite north wall of the Square was taken down to be recycled for use in the staircase, which led to the cancellation of the traditional New Year's Eve celebrations on grounds of both safety and lack of space. The real and permanent architectural loss was some of Barry's attractive red and white stone terrace, which had to be removed to accommodate the rise of the staircase. Admirals Cunningham, Beatty and Jellicoe were forced to seek shelter until the work was over and they could be reinstated, this time in closer formation towards the east of the remaining north wall.

The construction work offered an opportunity to install lifts for the disabled, a café and toilets beneath the terrace, opening out on to the square without intruding into the space. The welcome provision of toilets replaced an amenity taken away 20 years earlier when the entrances to the underground toilets at the southern edge fell victim to road widening.

The revitalised Square was officially reopened to the public on 2 July 2003 by the Mayor of London, Ken Livingstone, at a ceremony crowned by music, fireworks and the bells of St Martin's. Looking back on the project, the Mayor reflected:

Trafalgar Square is one of the world's most famous squares. As a place of celebration and protest it is rich in history and has been the scene of many memorable moments, from the VE Day celebrations in 1945, to the Celebrate South Africa concert with Nelson Mandela in 2001. Surrounded by some of London's iconic buildings, it is a landmark in its own right, but for many years was little better than a glorified roundabout, choked by traffic and pollution. I am proud of what we achieved in pedestrianising the north terrace and refurbishing the square, enhancing the experience of the millions who visit every year.

The changes to the Square prompt the question: who actually owns it? The short answer is that it is Crown land. The Queen in her capacity as the monarch, not as an individual, owns the subsoil by inalienable right, which means in practice that neither she nor her descendants can sell it. Permission to build tunnels or subways and lay underground pipes must be obtained from the Crown Estates. The task of managing the site formerly lay with the Commissioners of HM Woods, Forests and Land Revenues, and its various successors; today, it is the Greater London Authority's (GLA) responsibility.

OPPOSITE Visitors enjoying themselves on a warm summer day may not take very much interest in architectural awards, and yet the fact that they are there, in force, happily picnicking on the steps or chasing after the small band of pigeons still tolerated for sentimental reasons, must be part of the reason why 'World Squares For All: Trafalgar Square and its Environs' won the 2004 Royal Institute of British Architects award for Building in an Historic Context. As Jury Member Paul Velluet said: 'The winning project…has transformed and enlivened the role, function and accessibility of one of the country's best known and historically significant urban spaces with a series of related and substantial changes that are radical in concept, but sensitive to context'.

Julie Andrews' Mary Poppins may have sung about feeding the birds for 'tuppence a bag', but she probably did not have this in mind. Actress Judy Bowker, however, appears happy enough in this 1971 photograph.

After Barry's original square opened, people complained of litter and anti-social behaviour; since the revamp, wardens visibly patrol the area, which detracts a little from the sense of public ownership but which, according to surveys, has reduced not just litter and crime but also the fear of crime.

Not everyone was unreservedly enthusiastic about the latest changes. Architecture critic Hugh Pearman lamented:

[They] may be minor, but they give the place a strangely unbalanced air. Nelson's column with its four Landseer lions...forms a triangulated composition with the two great fountain pools by Sir Charles Barry...set on what was the half-way line of the square. Now that a great big staircase has been cut through what was previously the stone retaining wall on the north side – and is continued by the new terrace right up to the National Gallery – the upshot is that Trafalgar Square has changed shape. It has become visually much longer in the north–south direction. It is less contained. The fountains and Nelson consequently feel weirdly as if they have been shoved further south.

This, however, is thoughtful criticism, unlike some of the vituperative comments that were hurled at the Square in the nineteenth century.

One thing is for sure: the Square is cleaner and brighter than it has been in living memory, which, while initially down to a massive spring clean and the presence of the wardens and cleaners, owes much to the eviction of the main residents.

Dispersing the pigeons

'Could you please explain why you and the LCC [now the GLA] allow a stall permanently in Trafalgar square dispensing food for pigeons when we spend large sums in vainly trying to free our public buildings of the results?' This letter was written to the Office of Works in 1963, by a Mrs Whittier, and a defensive reply

The lamp-stand makes a convenient lookout perch for one of the four handsome Harris Hawks charged with the responsibility for keeping the Square's pigeons to a minimum. Native to the southern USA and most of South America, where it hunts in groups, the Harris Hawk is now the most popular bird of prey for falconers because it is easily trained, versatile, obliging and affectionate.

informed her that there was a public demand for having photographs taken while feeding the pigeons, just as in St Mark's Square, Venice.

Airborne rats or feathered friends, the thousands of feral pigeons at Trafalgar Square have long polarised the public. For every person who enjoyed feeding the birds there was another who complained of soiled clothes and probably more simply avoided the place altogether.

Some people were prepared to take matters into their own hands. The last of three generations of licensed pigeon food sellers, Bernard Rayner, contacted the police in 1996 when a mysterious character wearing a baseball cap and with a South London accent was discovered to be kidnapping hundreds of birds, allegedly for sale to restaurants. When Ken Livingstone decided the birds had had their day, yet another Battle of Trafalgar was about to begin with the Mayor and the GLA on one side and a loose coalition of animal rights activists and sentimentalists on the other. An Internet search for 'pigeons Trafalgar Square' produced around 11,000 hits, testifying to the level of interest.

An independent report commissioned by the Mayor advised that culling or egg removal would have no effect on numbers because incoming birds would take the vacant places. The only way of reducing numbers was to cut out or reduce the amount of food on offer.

Rayner accepted compensation for the revocation of his licence to sell bird food, and public feeding was discouraged before being prohibited in November 2003 under the by-laws. Outraged pigeon-lovers descended on the Square with sacks of grain, claiming that the birds would starve to death. A compromise was reached allowing for a gradual reduction in feeding which would give the birds time to relocate.

Four Harris Hawks named Nathan, Stripey, Squirt and – appropriately – Nelson were called up for active service, initially flying daily eight-hour missions in pairs to scare off regulars and newcomers. The cost brought more than a squawk from opposition members of the GLA who estimated that the programme, costing £106,000, worked out at nearly £30 per pigeon. The Mayor's spokesman riposted that the removal of the pigeons had allowed the Square to hold previously impossible revenue-generating events.

Artistic and social vision

The approach of the new millennium had encouraged many organisations to take stock of the past and look to the future. The National Gallery went ahead with a project to open up the ground-floor space of its East Wing and at the same time redevelop the Central Hall where the installation of humidity control in the latter allowed it to be used once again as a proper exhibition space.

A labyrinth of corridors and blind internal courtyards created in the East Wing by the various enlargements to the original building were opened up in September 2004 to create new visitor facilities in the form of an up-market café and shop. Accessible from the terrace through the Sir Paul Getty Entrance, they cater as much for casual visitors to the Square as for art lovers recharging their batteries. The Annenberg Court is another airy public space from which a great staircase rises against a dramatic black marble wall to lure even avowed philistines up to the Central Hall and into the presence of eight of the finest Renaissance works in the collection. The names given to the new extensions commemorate the latest in a long line of benefactors which began with Sir George Beaumont in 1823.

Long-term plans centre on the further development of the whole ground floor to accommodate the millions of visitors as well as providing further exhibition space. In 2005, the restored great staircase will be opened along with replacement of the existing toilets which the Gallery's director, Charles Saumarez Smith, felt would not be out of place in a Victorian prison. One day, perhaps, William Wilkins may get his great staircase up to the portico. George Agar Ellis, who so passionately advocated an easily

accessible, welcoming National Gallery with free admission and extensive opening hours, must surely be smiling with satisfaction.

The words in which Saumarez Smith summed up the recent and projected changes to his institution could quite easily be changed to fit any of the great buildings on the Square:

The National Gallery is adapting to the demands of its surroundings, transmogrifying itself in response to a changed urban dynamic. Like all great historic institutions, it is modernising itself, while, at the same time, I hope, remaining true to its original spirit. It is reinventing itself for a new millennium, while preserving and protecting its essential ethos as a nineteenth-century public gallery. It is performing the balancing act, which lies at the heart of any project of civic conservation, namely preserving the essential characteristics of a historic building, while, at the same time, allowing it to change and adapt to new uses, to the expectations and demands of what I understand as the spirit of the new urbanism, which tries to understand and interpret the mood of the city in terms of the complex demands and expectations of its human traffic, treating architecture as a living and breathing organism, rather than as a dead and passive mausoleum.

The most ambitious single plan, however, has come from St Martin-in-the-Fields, struggling to provide its Christian ministry,

'One of the most significant and worthwhile projects in London, making the buildings beautiful again and fit for service in the twenty-first century', is how Reverend Nicholas Holtam describes the proposed changes to one of the world's most famous churches. The stacked glass pavilion, seen here in this visualisation by Eric Parry Architects, provides the new entrance to the crypt.

For 40 years until it was irreparably damaged during the celebrations of England's win in the Rugby World Cup that culminated in Trafalgar Square, St Martin's displayed a Crib at Christmas. During 2004 a competition was held to design a replacement and the winner was announced in December. From 2005, Tomoaki Suzuki's wooden nativity figures, inspired by Italian Renaissance art and displayed in a Perspex enclosure, will be seen every Christmas in the Square to continue the tradition.

care for the disadvantaged, and cater for hundreds of thousands of music lovers and tourists – all within crumbling and inadequate accommodation. The old burial vaults in which so much of the social care has been provided are not just damp, cramped and, despite the best efforts of staff and clients, dismal by modern standards: they were actually declared unfit for the dead a century and a half ago.

Eric Parry Architects were selected from a short list of seven practices drawn from an international competition to design the scheme. Work is now beginning on a £34 million, three-year project to take out much of the old vaulted crypt and convert it into flexible, modern areas in which The Connection at St Martin's can carry out its pioneering role in social care and community

involvement. The musicians who usually rehearse in the vaults will get their own double-height rehearsal room, and a stacked glass entrance pavilion will provide visitors with easy access to the site. Not all the crypt is doomed: the café/restaurant will still retain the surroundings that help to make it so popular.

The church itself will gain from all this. The master plan will not only restore the fabric of the building but return the interior to something closer to James Gibbs' baroque original by stripping out many of the Victorian alterations. The proposed changes have provoked none of the cries of horror that usually greet any proposal to change a well-loved building. Fans of St Martin's probably share the view of P G Wodehouse that 'whatever may be said in favour of the Victorians, it is pretty generally admitted that

The day after US and British forces attacked targets in Afghanistan on 7 October 2001, supporters of the Stop the War Coalition gathered in Trafalgar Square to protest.

few of them were to be trusted within reach of a trowel and a pile of bricks', and will welcome work which paradoxically restores the church to an earlier age while making it fitter for the twenty-first century.

Nicholas Holtam, Vicar of St Martin's, views with affection the site on which his famous church stands:

> It has been a long time since St Martin's was in real fields. A former colleague, an American, said she thought we ought to rename ourselves 'St Martin's on the Block'. It's the paradoxes I love about this place: the church for those who are homeless and the Royal parish church; the parish church of the Admiralty and 'the peace church'; a church dedicated to St Martin, one of the patron saints of France, in a Square that remembers our greatest naval victory over the French. St Martin's is not a neat and tidy church but here it sits in one of the greatest squares in one of the greatest cities in the world, a place in which God is known.

Stop the War

The Gulf War in 1990–91, which followed Iraq's invasion of Kuwait, provoked protests only from committed pacifists. The War in Iraq, which actually began in March 2003, led to some of the largest demonstrations held at Trafalgar Square. Rallies aimed at averting an invasion began before redevelopment work on the Square would temporarily preclude such events: 27 September 2002 saw between 150,000 and 250,000 peaceful participants pack themselves into the space. A year later, the fifth major London protest took the form of a march from Hyde Park to the recently re-opened Square where the crowds heard passionate speeches by veteran campaigners, including Tony Benn whose address encapsulated not just his views on the war but the place that Trafalgar Square had come to occupy in the minds of many.

In May 2003 Admiral Nelson had some unexpected company when four pro-Tibet protestors scaled his Column without using harnesses. Three unfurled a banner of the exiled Dalai Lama and then abseiled down. The fourth, a professional stuntman, jumped off, opening his parachute and landing safely.

Double gold medallist, Kelly Holmes, and her team
mates were cheered to the heavens at a victory parade
in Trafalgar Square after their triumphant return from
the 2004 Athens Olympics.

All the flamboyance of Bollywood came to the steps of Trafalgar Square in a July 2004 dance spectacular, just one of many arts events staged throughout the summer. Simmy Gupta choreographed the new commission in which dancers explored the architecture and energy of public spaces using movement, colour and water.

The first time I came to this square was 50 years ago when Eden launched war against Egypt. A few months later Eden was out. I was here in 1964 in support of 'terrorist' Nelson Mandela, and here for the poll tax, and many other demos. Trafalgar Square is the real parliament of the country.

Not all recent protests have been on such a scale. On 21 April 2002 Neil Herron addressed supporters and curious passers-by at what he called 'The Crown Pound and Democracy Rally' in support of the shopkeepers prosecuted for selling produce only in imperial rather than metric measures. He told his audience:

> The police do not look for a 1.85-metre tall, 90-kilogram man in connection with a robbery. It's 6 feet and 15 stone. Nobody gets stabbed with a 142.4-millimetre knife. It's 6 inches. Beckham didn't score that goal from 22.3 metres. It was 25 yards…

Despite the traditional demonstrations and publicity stunts, Trafalgar Square is changing its image, and rapidly. As the pigeons have been forced out, the public has been enticed in. South Africa Day brings in the crowds to shout with joy, not anger; art is not confined to the National Gallery, it can be an ephemeral pyramid of bananas bemusing pedestrians, a sculpture exhibition at Canada House, paintings by clients of St Martin's or a crowd of artists of all ages creating a giant copy of Constable's *Haywain*. Vivaldi and Handel at St Martin-in-the-Fields co-exist rather than compete with Nitin Sawhney and the Pet Shop Boys. But for the rain, Puccini's *La Bohème* would have tugged a few heartstrings in summer 2004. Diwali and Christmas both fill the Square with light. The space is unashamedly populist, but it always has been; what

it has gained is a marriage of relaxation and vibrancy. Visitors of every age, race, creed, political persuasion and colour happily stroll and picnic among heroes of the former British Empire, a profligate king, a dethroned monarch and a slave-owning US president. It welcomes the New Year reveller and the committed protestor; the rugby supporter and the music fan. It will continue to invite controversy, the latest being whether a proposed 9-foot statue of Nelson Mandela is too large for the terrace of the National Gallery or whether the Square should remain a place of honour for the British. The debate at least proves that people care enough about the place to become passionate.

As early as 1914, a paper was read to RIBA suggesting the wholesale redevelopment of the Square and the buildings around it, including the removal of Nelson's Column and the fountains. A few days later a long editorial in *The Times* of 21 May responded.

> It would be a very handsome place…but it would not be Trafalgar Square. Trafalgar Square means something quite different from the finest square in the world, which our architects could doubtless make it if they had the chance… The value of the 'show places' in a great and ancient city does not lie wholly in their artistic beauty…

Certainly Trafalgar Square has neither the style of Milan's Piazza del Duomo, nor the architectural glory of Venice's St Mark's Square – although it can at least boast far fewer pigeons than the latter; it has less space than Place de La Concorde, and still too much traffic. Architecturally and aesthetically it is something of a 'dog's dinner', and the finest views, the ones that give it a sense of unified grandeur, are best obtained from a hot air balloon. It isn't even square. But it is Trafalgar Square.

It is arguable that Trafalgar Square would have benefited from a single vision instead of many different ones reflecting the changing preoccupations of their respective periods. But architecture's loss has most definitely been history's gain.

BIBLIOGRAPHY

Official records relating to Trafalgar Square can be found at the National Archives at Kew, Surrey. For the most part, those relevant to this book came from the records of the files of the Office of Works and the Office of Land Revenue Records and Enrolments. Some material was also found in other files such as the records of the Metropolitan Police. Readers interested in delving into these fascinating and far from dry records can visit www.catalogue.nationalarchives.gov.uk. By searching using terms such as 'Trafalgar Square', 'National Gallery' or 'Charing Cross', for example, a wealth of references can be obtained before visiting the Archives, requesting material by post or employing a researcher.

Books, periodicals, articles and newspapers

Amos, Charles, 'On the Government Waterworks in Trafalgar Square' in Charles Manby and James Forrest (eds) *Minutes of Proceedings of the Inst. Of Civil Engineers,* W Clowes and Sons, 1862.

Anonymous rioters, *Poll Tax Riot,* ACAB Press, 1990.

Architect Engineer and Surveyor.

Art Monthly.

Automatic Electric Company Ltd, *Electro-matic Vehicle-Actuated Signals* (no date).

Blackwood, John, *London's Immortals,* Savoy Press, 1989.

Bosanquet, Helen, *Social Work in London,* Harvester Press, 1973.

Canada High Commission, *Canada House,* 1998.

Canada High Commission, *Canada In London – An Unofficial Glimpse of Canada's Sixteen High Commissioners 1880–1980,* 1980.

Clarke, Sir George, *The Royal College of Physicians of London,* Clarendon Press for the Royal College of Physicians, 1966.

Cooper, Leonard, *Sir Henry Havelock KCB,* Bodley Head, 1957.

Copcutt, James, *The Hon. Major Fitzmaurice's Grand Oxy-Olifiant Life-Light, as used to illuminate the royal fleet etc,* Edward West, 1859.

Country Life, *The Lutyens memorial,* Country Life, 1950.

Daily Mail.

Darke, Joe, *Monument Guide to England and Wales,* Macdonald, 1991.

Davenport G, McDonald I and Moss-Gibbons C, *The Royal College of Physicians and its Collections,* James and James, 2001.

Davis, Lieut. Colonel Nathaniel Newnham, *Dinners and Diners – how and where to dine in London,* Grant Richards, 1899/1901.

Davis, Terence, *John Nash,* David and Charles, 1973.

Friedman, Terry, *James Gibbs,* Yale, 1984.

Gordon, Gilbert A H, *The Rules of the Game – Jutland and British Naval Command,* John Murray, 1996.

Guardian, The.

Gunnis, Rupert Forbes, *Dictionary of British Sculptors 1660–1851,* Odhams Press, 1953.

Gurney, Christabel, 'When the Boycott began to Bite History' in *Today,* June 1999.

Gwilt, Joseph, *Observations on the communication of Mr Wilkins to the editor of the Athenaeum relative to the National Gallery,* privately printed, 1838.

Gwilt, Joseph, *Project for a National Gallery on the site of Trafalgar Square, Charing Cross,* privately printed, 1838.

Illustrated London News.

Independent, The.

Jackson, Peter, *George Scharf's London: sketches and watercolours of a changing city 1820–1850,* John Murray, 1987.

Lady's Newspaper.

Loughton J K, *The Nelson Memorial,* George Allan, 1986.

Mace, Rodney, *Trafalgar Square – Emblem of Empire,* Lawrence and Wishart, 1976.

Macnab, Roy, *The Story of South Africa House,* J Ball, Johannesburg, 1923.

Marriott, Leo, *What's Left Of Nelson,* Dial, 1995.

McCamley, N J, *Saving Britain's Art Treasures,* Lee Cooper, 2003.

Morris, William, *Death Song for Alfred Linnell,* privately printed, 1887.

Munk, William, *Roll of the Royal College of Physicians Of London,* volume 3, Royal College of Physicians, 1878.

Murphy, C W, 'I Live in Trafalgar Square' (song) Francis, Day and Hunter, 1902.

Parson's Magazine, Nelson Centenary Edition, 1905.

Observer, The.

Ormond, Richard, *Sir Edwin Landseer,* Thames and Hudson, 1981.

Oxford University Press, *Dictionary of National Biography,* 2004 (available online at many public libraries).

Pennick, Nigel, *Tunnels Under London,* Fenris-Wolf, 1981.

Phoenix Assurance Company, *A History of the Phoenix Assurance Company,* 1915.

Porter, Dale H, *The Life and Times of Sir Goldsworthy Gurney, gentleman, scientist and inventor, 1793–1875,* Associated University Press, c. 1998.

Punch.

Purser, Charles, *The Prospects of the Nation in Regards to its National Gallery,* Cochrane and McCrone, 1833.

Pyne, William, and Coombe, William, *Microcosm of London,* R Ackermann, 1808–11.

Read, Benedict, *Victorian Sculpture,* Yale, 1982.

Report of the Select Committee appointed to inquire into the Plan sanctioned by the Commissioners of the Woods and Forests for the laying out the vacant space in Trafalgar Square, published 17/6/1840.

Royal Institute of British Architects, *Battle of Styles,* 1975.

Rome, R C, *The Union Club,* Batsford, 1948.

South Africa High Commission, *Report for South Africa House,* December 1965.

South Africa High Commission, *South Africa House in the Making,* (no date).

Sala, George Augustus, *London Up To Date,* A & C Black, 1895.

Saunders, A, *St. Martin-in-the-Fields,* St Martin-in-the-Fields, (no date).

Smith, Henry Louis, *Address…Presenting a copy in bronze of the Houdon statue of George Washington from the Commonwealth of Virginia…,* 1921.

Socialist Review.

London County Council, *Survey of London,* volume 20, 1940.

Sugden, John, *Nelson: a Dream of Glory,* Jonathan Cape, 2004.

Summerson, Sir John, *Life and Work of John Nash, Architect,* Allen and Unwin, 1980.

Sun Alliance and London Insurance Group, *Trafalgar Square Branch 1726–1970* (copy in Westminster Archives).

Taylor, Brandon, *Art for the Nation* Manchester University Press, 1999.

Taylor, George Ledwell, *The Autobiography of an Octogenarian Architect, being a record of his studies at home and abroad* privately printed, 1870–2.

The Grand Hotel (handbook for guests), c. 1888.

Times, The.

Turvey, Ralph, *The Economics of Real Property,* Allen and Unwin, 1967.

Teahan, John Patrick, Unpublished Diaries Accession Number 19950023-001, the George Metcalf Archival Collection, Canadian War Museum.

Walker, Richard, *The Nelson Portraits* Royal Naval Museum Publications, c. 1998.

Wandsworth Guardian.

Wilkins, William, *On the Change in the Line of the Front of the Buildings for the National Gallery* (see Gwilt, *Observations…),* (no date).

Winton, John, *Cunningham – The Greatest Admiral since Nelson,* John Murray, 1998.

Wyatt, M C, *Prospectus of a model to the memory of Lord Nelson,* privately printed, 1809.

General Websites:

www.bbc.co.uk

www.cnduk.org

www.iwm.org.uk

www.london.gov.uk

www.met.police.uk

www.royal-navy.mod.uk

www.nationalgallery.org.uk

www.victorianlondon.org

Specific Websites

www.fathom.com 'London Electricity on Show: Spectacular Events in Victorian London' in association with the Science Museum.

www.cwgcuser.org.uk 'Analysis of casualty and Fatality Figures' (casualties associated with London Underground in the Second World War) by Nick Cooper.

www.sovereignty.org.uk Speech by Neil Herron, Metric Martyr at the Crown, Pound and Democracy Rally .

www.princeofwales.gov.uk HRH The Prince of Wales's speech to the Royal Institute of British Architects.

http://users.argonet.co.uk/users/ken.mcnaught/ironm.html 'The Harry Bensley Story' by Ken McNaught.

www.casebook.org/ripper 'Jack the Ripper: Person or persons unknown' by Gary Wroe, 1995.

www.nhm.ac.uk 'New Fossil find adds to growing evidence of life in London during the Ice Age' (National History Museum).

www.oldbaileyonline.org Proceedings of the Old Bailey late seventeenth to early nineteenth century.

www.388thbg.org 'Remembering VE Day' by Bill Rellstab (The 388th Anthology Vols 1-2).

www.rsa.org.uk 'The Fourth Plinth' (Royal Society of Arts).

http://www.forces.gc.ca/hr/dhh/Downloads/cmhq/cmhq005.pdf Report of Major C P Stacey, Historical Officer, stationed at the Canadian High Commission during the Second World War.

PICTURE CREDITS

Front Jacket: Hulton-Deutsch Collection/Corbis; 2 Rob Brimson/Getty Images; 8,9,10&11L From the Private Collection of Pentland Group plc; 11R Jean Hood; 12 London Aerial Photo Library/Corbis; 13&14 Antiquarian Images; 15 Angelo Hornak/Corbis; 16 George Scharf/Copyright of The Trustees of The British Museum/Ref: 1862-6-14-105; 17 Ash Rare Books; 18 Bearsted Collection, Upton House, Warwickshire www.bridgeman.co.uk 19 Historical Picture Archive/Corbis; 20 Kings Mews, Charing Cross from Ackermann's "Microcosm of London", Rowlandson, T. (1956-1827) & Pugin, A. C. (1762-1832) Private Collection/www.bridgeman.co.uk; 21 Joseph Anton Couriguer/National Portrait Gallery; 22T Antiquarian Images; 22B William Daniell, after George Dance/National Portrait Gallery; 23 By kind permission of the Canadian High Commission; 25&27 Ash Rare Books/Shepherd (Thomas Hosmer); 28 The Royal College of Physicians of London; 29 John Nash/Guildhall Library/Corporation of London; 30 George Scharf/Copyright of The Trustees of The British Museum/Ref: 1862-6-14-10; 31 George Scharf/Copyright of The Trustees of The British Museum/Ref: 1862-6-14-96; 32 George Scharf/Copyright of The Trustees of The British Museum/Ref: 1862-6-14-7; 33 Michael Rysbrack/V&A Images/Victoria & Albert Museum; 34 Ackerman's "Microcosm of London", engraved by Joseph Constantine Stadler (fl. 1780-1812), 1809 (aquatint), Rowlandson, T. (1756-1827) & Pugin, AC (1762-1832) The Stapleton Collection/www.bridgeman.co.uk; 36 View from Charing Cross looking towards the Strand, 1842 (litho), Boys, Thomas Shotter (1803-74)/Guildhall Library, Corporation of London/www.bridgeman.co.uk; 38 Frederick MacKenzie/V&A Images/Victoria & Albert Museum; 40&41 © National Gallery London; 42 Cross-readings at Charing Cross/Guildhall Library, Corporation of London/www.bridgeman.co.uk; 44 ©National Gallery, London; 45 © Illustrated London News Picture Library; 46 E. J. Brewtnall/The Mansell Collection/Getty Images; 47 From the Private Collection of Pentland Group plc; 48 © Illustrated London News Picture Library; 49 Michael Nicholson/Corbis; 50 © Illustrated London News Picture Library; 51 RIBA Library Drawings Collection; 53 Royalty Free/© Illustrated London News Picture Library; 54 Edward Pether/Museum of London; 55 Photolibrary.com; 56 The Mansell Collection/Getty Images; 57BL&BC © Illustrated London News Picture Library; 58 Hulton/Getty Images; 59 © Illustrated London News Picture Library; 60 From the Private Collection of Pentland Group plc; 61 William Frederick/City of Westminster City Archives Centre; 62 London Stereoscopic Company/Getty Images; 63&64 V&A Images/Victoria & Albert Museum; 65 © Illustrated London News Picture Library; 66 Guildhall Library, Corporation of London; 68 Pickersgill, Henry William (1782-1875) Private Collection, Philip Mould, Historical Portraits Ltd, London www.bridgeman.co.uk; 69 Jan Buchofsky-Houser/Corbis; 71 Guildhall Library, Corporation of London; 72 Canaletto, (Giovanni Antonio Canal) (1697-1768) Private Collection/www.bridgeman.co.uk; 73 Mary Evans Picture Library; 74 City of Westminster City Archives Centre; 75 © Illustrated London News Picture Library; 77 RIBA Library Drawings Collection; 78 Patrick Loobey Collection; 79 www.bridgeman.co.uk; 80 City of Westminster City Archives Centre; 81 © Illustrated London News Picture Library; 82 By permission of The Imperial War Museum Q53219; 83 By permission of The Imperial War Museum Q31083; 84 A. F. Kersting/Chrysalis Image Library; 85 E. O. Hoppé/Corbis; 86L&TR By Permission of Canadian High Commission; 87 Hulton/Getty Images; 88L Hulton/Getty Images; 88R Museum of London Picture Library; 89 TNA:PRO ref.20/180; 91 Hulton/Getty Images; 92&93 Hulton-Deutsch Collection/Corbis; 94 Royalty Free/© Illustrated London News Picture Library; 95 Eves, Reginald-Grenville (1876-1941) The Crown Estate/www.bridgeman.co.uk; 97 © National Gallery, London; 98 Hulton/Getty Images; 100 Hulton-Deutsch Collection/Corbis; 102 TNA:PRO ref.21/291; 104 © Illustrated London News Picture Library; 105 © popperfoto.com; 106 Hulton-Deutsch Collection/Corbis; 107 Bettman/Corbis; 108 By kind permission of The Royal Bank of Scotland Group plc; 109 By permission of The Canadian High Commission; 110 Hulton/Getty Images; 111 Hulton-Deutsch Collection/Corbis; 112 By kind permission of Rev Nicholas Holtam; 113 © National Gallery, London; 114 Angelo Hornak/Corbis; 116 Jeremy Horner/Corbis; 118&119 Hulton-Deutsch Collection/Corbis; 120 AFP/Getty Images; 121 Reuters/Corbis; 122&123 Howard Davies/Corbis; 125 Cass Sculpture Foundation; 126 Nigel Young/Foster & Partners; 128 Mirrorpix Picture Library; 129 Ian Waldie/Getty Images; 131&132 By kind permission of Rev Nicholas Holtam; 133 Sion Touhig/Getty Images; 134 Reuters/Corbis; 135 Tom Shaw/Getty Images; 136 By permission of The Greater London Authority; 138/9 Jeremy Walker/Getty Images.

INDEX

Numbers in *italics* indicate captions.